# So You Want to be a Successful Writer

# E.R. Vernor

Cover art and design by E.R. Vernor

*So You Want to be a Successful Writer,* E.R. Vernor

ISBN-13: 978-1507628324

Published by

Dark Moon Press

P.O. Box 11496

Fort Wayne, Indiana 46858-1496

www.DarkMoonPress.com

DarkMoon@DarkMoonPress.com

# Table of Contents

# About the Author

Eric Vernor is an expert on showing people how to identify and maximize their natural strengths for success in life. Requested for motivational speaking at schools, bookstores and business. A speaker, consultant and writer for over 10 years, Eric has presented at Universities, bookstores and conventions in Buffalo, Indianapolis, Atlanta, Las Vegas and many more cities on various topics. He is the author/co-author of more than 30 books.

He has lectured at conventions and universities, and radio. He currently the publisher of Dark Moon Press and CEO of Dark Moon Productions.

The author enjoys painting and movies while not writing, and has degrees in business management and criminal justice.

# Dedication

I dedicate the book to the writers that inspired me when I first began my career, Michelle Belanger, and Gavin Baddeley, and to all of the people who have supported me over the years. To Starr Morgayne, who dug my first manuscript out of the trash and insisted I keep at it, my biggest cheerleader and devoted friend. To my fans and friends, I could not have done this without you.

# Introduction

I want you to be successful as a writer. I remember the feeling of putting out my first book; the excitement it brought, the happiness of having it in my own hands and looking it over. But then the fear kicked in. How do I sell this, this four foot square heap of paper and ink? You may not have that burden. You may in fact have a bigger one. You see, once my pallet was sold out I had earned my investment back with profit and it was done. But then I decided to add more books to it and reprint it, and bring other authors onboard to share my vision, with you. But the fear is still there, how do I make a living off what I love to do you are asking. I am about to open the black curtain and let you in on my decade of trial and error. I thought I would share a decade of insights on how to sell more books, a real heart to heart. This is lengthy because it did not happen overnight for me. I had mentors in business and public speaking. Presentation is everything; it is part acting and know how to act – as in how to behave. Without it you are just a product maker and not getting people enthused about your work and you will not make money.

Let's not kid ourselves, we create for two reasons. One, because it is a part of ourselves and two, we want to make a living; the more the better! It has been taboo to talk about money but it shouldn't be, and writers make their feelings known to me, as a publisher, when I go to conventions. I hear the complaints and strive to fix the issues so that I stand out from the rest of the publishers.

Being a Writer

Like a lot of people, I fell into my calling. I had always been an avid reader; ever since I was a small boy I voraciously devoured every book in my grandfather's library. His collection ran from the original *Hardy Boys* detective series from the 1950's, extensive encyclopedias, and classics like *The Swiss Family Robinson* and *Black Beauty*. What later shaped my own genre of interest was Edgar Allan Poe's *Tale Tell Heart* and Greek Mythology. At age ten, a neighbor loaned me *The Hobbit* and *The Lord of the Rings*. Immediately after that, many trips to the library expanded my joy of reading with books like Mary Shelley's *The Modern Prometheus* (known to many as Frankenstein) and Bram Stoker's *Dracula*.

My young adult life was filled with various menial jobs and I was far from satisfied with the work I was doing.

During the same time as working for a book distribution company, and watching other people's life's work go by me on a conveyor belt, I was working part time at a small local New Age/Occult/Goth clothing store. A great many of the local Goths and Pagans would come in and complain about how they were treated by the general public for being alternative. I know how it felt for me to be ostracized for being different when I was a child and I got the idea to write something allowing people from many subcultures to speak out about this topic. Now, at this time, it was a bit of a whim to work at it little by little so that I could use it as possibly a newsletter or series of articles for publication but, when I injured myself on the job and was forced to convalesce after the surgery I mentally shifted gears. My writings went from short articles to an entire book. I dove into the history of Gothic literature, world history that tied in with my subjects, and decided to make it into my first book, *Embracing the Darkness: Understanding Dark Subcultures*.

Like so many people who were new to writing, I had no idea what to do with my work when I finished it. Keep in mind, in 2004 self-publishing wasn't at the same level of acceptance. Such methods were considered the desperate last resorts of people not able to be taken on by legitimate publishers.

I sought out *The Writers Market* books which are still a great resource for writers. I learned about cover letters, finding agents, and the massive lists of publishers in the book.

When I was mulling over sending it to a major publishing house, I was torn between keeping the integrity of the book's content as it was written versus the editors mighty red pen deciding what stayed or went. I did finally get up the courage to send it to a rather large publishing house. I was excited and nervous the whole time. When I received a response from the publisher they felt that my manuscript needed toned down. They said that it was too academic for their readers. I was disappointed and thought maybe I just wasn't good enough to be a published writer. With the encouragement of my loved ones, I didn't give up. After much thought I finally decided to go ahead and publish the book myself. I was not aware of print-on-demand at that point in time so I contacted a printer and was given a quote for a thousand copies to be printed. I scraped together the necessary funds to do so and a month or so later a semi pulled up to drop off a pallet of books. That's right, a pallet, four feet wide, and four feet tall. Case after case of books, fifty at a time, were carried into the building. The sheer joy of opening the first box and holding in my hands a physical copy of my very first book was indescribable. To this day, I remember that moment, and even though getting copies of each new book feels like winning a trophy, the first time was the most meaningful. Since that day I have written over two dozen titles and spoken at colleges and conventions on, not only the subject of writing, but also, publishing. But I am getting a bit ahead of myself here.

It took me two years to self-promote and sell off that first thousand copies. I will never forget arranging the bookstore signings at Little Professor and Borders (I still miss that store) and meeting people who wanted to listen to the lecture. When people asked me to sign copies, I knew I found my calling.

I am happy I self-published. Had I not, I would not have learned the inside daily workings of publishing and it has helped launch other people's writing careers. Like being a writer in the first place, I never set out to be a publisher for a living, but as I kept putting out my own work, I discovered others who didn't know what to do or felt that larger companies had too many flaws.

As time went on, and I had already published several books of my own and others, a radio host that had become friends with me let me know Schiffer Publishing was looking for new materials and he put me in touch with his editor. After our initial talk, I decided to put my most current project at the time out with Schiffer.

I held the contract, signed it, and hesitated to mail it out. It was odd, I was torn once again; wondering if I was betraying my values of doing everything myself. At the same time, I wanted to confirm in myself that I was worth my salt as a writer, and have a sense of validity that I was not just able to be out there by simply printing copies and selling to the same fan base that was loyal to me. However, friends convinced me that it wasn't the case, as at this point I had already gained sales of my work in Brazil, the UK, and even China. A man coming back from the war in Iraq told me my first book was in the tent library and he was shocked to see I was from his hometown. At this point, I realized I had actually reached a new level in my career.

Getting a copy of *Cemetery Gates Death and Mourning through the Ages*, my first book in full color by another company that was much larger and well established was parallel to getting my first book. A couple years later, my first hardcover book, *Zombie Nation From Myth to Modern Frenzy*, through Schiffer, was another pinnacle point. I have maintained writing via Dark Moon Press at the same time, as well as various magazines and Yahoo groups to spread my name, and have grown to doing massive conventions, such as Scarefest, ConVocation, and DragonCon, as a speaker and panelist for subjects I write about. My decade of work felt worth it, and being self-employed for many years made me satisfied I made the right decision.

I meet a lot of the people who ask about being an author. By and large, they aren't necessarily dreaming of hitting the big time, at least not initially. Most are simply interested in seeing their work out in print. But others dream big, and want to do it as a profession, and to build a career as a writer as I have. My authors at Dark Moon Press ask me questions and I started a newsletter to them to coach them to get more sales. I noticed as they put what I had done into action, some of them did indeed get more copies sold, so I knew it was time I wrote this book to help more people follow in my footsteps.

It is my hope that sharing what I have been doing, the resources contained in this book and various methods of getting attention will bring you the same satisfaction I feel.

There are many aspects you need to consider before jumping straight into printing and selling your first book, that I feel is necessary to understand in order to become successful.

*Realities and mindset*

As a realist and educator, I am full of positive advice and want to share with you the greatness that can come from being a self-employed, world traveling individual who takes joy in signing books for hundreds of fans per year, I know I love every bit of the upside to the job! However, I don't believe in sugar coating and hiding from the realities of the profession, as it is always hardest at the beginning. Before you start out thinking it is easy to turn the page and start a new career to quick riches and international fame, let me caution you that every successful author has had to struggle to get known. I am certainly not discouraging anyone from following in my footsteps, not at all. In fact, this course is giving you the short cuts I wish I had over a dozen years or so ago! But, let's get the realities that aren't as enjoyable out of the way first. In knowing what some of the rough spots are ahead of time, we can understand and plan around most of them!

One of the most critical things to acknowledge is important to understand is your own mental makeup that is to say, you have to need to do it. I know a lot of authors, in varying stages of what might be deemed successful writers who say the truly feel didn't have any other choices. Deep down, they always seemed to know it was a part of them, like me reading and working with books at Ingram, that they have always feel a need to write.

Just doing it is not enough however. You have to be mentally tough. There's so much rejection in writing, so many projects that fall through, hopes that are dashed, etc. that you must have a thick skin and a strong resolve to make it really work. You well and truly have to love it or it'll drive you crazy. The stress and work that goes into it, even after you are done writing the book, just might regardless!

Ask yourself, and be honest, are you truly cut out to write for a living? Are you willing to take rejection? Can you handle bad reviews on sites like Amazon.com? Are you focused enough to prove to yourself and the demanding world that wants your next book after a mere weekend of reading your latest, even though it took you months or even years to write it in the first place, that you can do it? It happens, all the time. Are you dedicated enough to stay up half the night pounding out your manuscript while the rest of the world sleeps? Keep in mind, you may have family that makes demands on your time, dating, and yes, a day job. Can you dedicate yourself to maintaining your life and work to pay your bills while still forcing yourself to stay inside on a nice bright sunny day, when others are enjoying their time off work, to pursue a dream of leaving the day job?

You have to truly need and want to write, because, to be perfectly honest, there are always easier, more enjoyable distractions, like going on vacation. The desire to write has to be a part of you, for it will become a very large part of your life.

People ask me all the time what's it like being a writer, and most folks have the opinion that you are rich because you are a known name, basking in the glory of attention between feverishly working on a project. While you may enjoy it, and yes, the attention is a greatly satisfying aspect of it, keep in mind several sayings:

*Being a writer is a fast way to very slow money*. It took me eight years to feel confident enough to leave a good job that had stability and benefits, to take the plunge into being a writer full time.

*Do what you love and the money will follow.* It may sound cliché, but clichés exist because they contain a lot of truth to them. Gene Simmons said many times "find a way to make your hobby your full time job, and then you will be truly happy doing what you love for an income". I was reminded of the saying, if you do what you love you will never 'work' a day in your life. I agree to a point – but it is work. In fact, being a full time writer is more than a full time job, because, as you will learn here, once the book is written the real work starts! Nobody told me in the early days that marketing a book, once written, is where the fun stops. We will cover all of those needed aspects in this book, as I share everything I have learned.

*You are only as good as your last book.* Even when you reach, what you feel is, success, it is like being an actor or anything else, your next project will continue to define you, and there is no resting on one's laurels. Yes, I hang framed posters of some of my book covers on my office wall, but it is not merely a trophy to enjoy, rather, it is a push to continue to reach a better level of accomplishment. Try to compete with yourself, not others.

It starts slow. Very few are able to write a book or two and become the next Stephen King, or any world known best seller, who gets an advance royalty check for more money than most Americans make in a year. Even established writers take years to live well off the decision of being a writer.

How do successful people become successful? They do things. Success doesn't just happen; you have to fight for it. Be the Rocky Balboa of your own inner struggle to the top. Champions just go out and do what they need to do.

Your books are a product. You, as an author, become a brand as well, especially when you write for a genre repeatedly. My book *Unlocking the Secrets of Control, Wealth, and Power* details a lot of this and I am using some of the most relevant aspects of it here in this work, but please read the other when you finish this course!

There are people and learning resources to help with the things you do not know how to do or that you do not want to do on your own. Most of my education came from various books on self-help, motivational speaking, and college courses on business (because you are a business when you work for yourself) but you have to push yourself and allow success to come. That's right. We are often our own biggest roadblocks to success. You have to allow it to come instead of doubting yourself.

When someone is waiting for success, they often fail because they do not have confidence in their ability to do go after it full bore. The way to get confidence in your ability to do something is to simply do it, feel the accomplishment of all the efforts come into being, or learn from the mistakes you make. The way to get that confidence is not to look to someone else; you cannot hold yourself up to others who have already reached the potential you may have. Instead, use your idols as goals, learn from them in what they do, how they speak, their confidence and what happens when they put out a new book. You can learn a lot from the mistakes of others to avoid doing them yourself, and it saves you the heartache and wasted time.

Although I am very happy about the success I have had, I'd like to stress that I don't have all the answers, and the other writers I know will tell you that they don't know all the answers either. The books I write most likely will never see the *New York Times* best-seller list, at least until I throw myself into fiction with a big publisher one of these days – I can dream anyway.

Having a great idea is only the first step, though. Ideas are not worth anything until you put them into action.

Putting ideas into action is where many people stumble. They may be afraid to try something new, or are confused about how to get started.

Or they may think they do not have the skills or resources necessary to make their idea successful.

Here is a simple three step plan for going from idea to action:

*Make a plan and write it down.* A big project is less intimidating when you break it into a series of small steps. If you are not sure where to start, work backwards. For example, if your project is to create and sell a new product online, one of the last steps might be to make sales. What do you have to do before that? You need to have a sales page on a website, a way to accept payments, and the product itself. What steps will you have to take to put those things in place? Keep working backwards until you reach the beginning.

If you are not sure what needs to be done, then your first step is to learn. Identify the resources available to teach you what you need to know or the people who can help you.

Put dates with each of the steps in your plan to keep yourself moving along.

Forget fear. Do not let fear stop you from getting started. Do not worry about what other people will think if you fail. Anyone who would criticize someone for trying and failing probably doesn't have the nerve to try anything themselves, so forget about them. Besides, you are not going to fail. With your plan in place, you will succeed.

Now for what everyone *needs* to hear but so very few of us *want* to hear. The bad side.

*The good side of being a writer!*

Having accidentally become a writer has certainly had its positives in my life. I never was one for doing the nine to five banker or factory job, it killed my creative spirit. I love being at home where things are cozy and familiar as well as making my own hours. Now, you would think that would make me lazy and slack off, but in my case, I became a

14

workaholic for several reasons. I love what I do. I have hundreds of ideas, and every time I put a few books out and say I have no more ideas left in me, a topic of discussion or an article or movie will come along and put a thought into my head that becomes a book.

I also enjoy venturing out after weeks or months of my self-imposed exile and seeing the world. As introverted as I am, it is nice to see friends (in my case, doing conventions is a great excuse to get out and see people I haven't seen for a year or more). Conventions, are fun because you get to see the booths of merchandise and the stars as well as meet fans. There is something highly satisfying when people hand you a book to sign; and the money can be good. Just keep in mind that your trips are part of the business of being who you are and be sure and factor in the costs such as tables at the event (unless you are an invited guest and they provide it for you), your food and hotel, and gas or flight, bus, train or whatever method of transportation you opt for to get to each place.

Just like any other profession, it was a struggle years ago, and still is if you don't have the insights and guidance of what to do. I have sold thousands and thousands of my titles to fans as far away as China, the UK, and Malaysia. This is why I'm offering you the things that I have learned from experience.

From early on in my career, I was terrified to speak in front of a few people, now I do it before several hundred, often, so I am teaching people how to overcome stage fright. Worried about booking yourself? Not a problem. I cover how to do a successful book launch that gets you radio interviews, store signings, speaking engagements at conventions and universities, and how to get endorsements for your work. I go into great detail on all the aspects between self-publishing to traditional publishing and inside information on proper layout and formatting and design to get a great book in the hands of your readers.

I want you to start thinking differently about what it means to be a successful author in today's world. My goal is to help you build your platform before you launch a new book, so that when you do launch, it's an instant success. Some of the topics will be formatting, submitting to publishers, the pros and cons of self-publishing vs. small publisher vs. large publisher, if you need an agent and how to find them, your websites, a lot of information on social media use, public speaking, store signing tips, mass distribution, Amazon and Barnes and Noble, designing and formatting do's and don'ts, finding editors, reviews, and handling rejection. I also go deep into how to dress, how to plan out a book signing tour, and a lot more. You'll have lots of pdf files to keep, quizzes, and videos to watch as I interview other writers to add their perspective. I also have graphic designers and editors sharing a wealth of information.

I mentioned the word "bestseller" several times. What does that mean exactly? The word "bestseller" can be hard to define. Do I mean a #1 New York Times bestseller? Or an in-the-Top-10-of-some-obscure-Amazon-category bestseller?

In a way, calling anything an Instant Bestseller is a bit tongue-in-cheek. If you've read anything I've written on bestseller lists, I'm not a fan of considering a book successful just because it made it onto a certain list.

A good friend of mine has sold more than 150,000 copies of their book in its first year and netted a six-figure contract, yet her book and many books that sell just as well never hit the New York Times bestseller list. In fact, most never sell more than 10,000 or 15,000 copies. I think we can all agree that 150,000 copies is a successful book!

There are three options authors have when it comes to launching a new book:

*Write and hope.* I've launched my book! But because I haven't prepared for the launch by creating an author platform, all I can do is hope it sells. Worse yet, I wrote a book, put it on Amazon myself without knowing industry standards of publishing and have no fan base to even sell it to!

*Write and pay.* I've launched my book! But because I haven't prepared by creating an author platform, I now throw a lot of money at advertising and publicity, if I can sort through the sharks that will fleece me out of money to try to force the sale of a few copies.

*Write and know.* Because I've prepared by creating my author platform ahead of time, I'm now confidently launching my new book—and I already know it will sell well.

The third option is why I created this course.

I want you to have that third option—and all the confidence and book sales that result.

It doesn't really matter which bestseller list you hit, or if you ever even get on a list. What matters is launching a book to an audience that's excited to read it.

Here's the author life you want: Even before I pen the first word of my next book, I know I have an audience ready to buy it. I'm already connected to enough of those fans that I know the book will be successful from Day One.

When I launched my first book, *Embracing the Darkness Understanding Dark Subcultures,* it was overwhelming seeing 1,000 copies stacked up and thinking how am I ever going to sell them all? But in just two years I had done just that. Imagine what you can do with all that I have learned since then at your fingertips! What took me years to learn you will learn in just a few months' time!

Now as I begin work on my thirty-second book, I know that I will be able to launch bigger than ever because I'm already directly connected to my fans.

I've not only created a successful book-selling platform for myself, I've also created them for dozens of my authors I publish over the last few years.

Writing an amazing book is only half of the 'equation' to becoming a successful author. You could have written the greatest book in the world... but if no one knows who you are, where to find you online, or if they can even trust that your book is worth reading... then it is extremely difficult to sell a lot of books.

How would it change your writing career if . . .

You were directly connected to thousands of your fans and could reliably communicate with them and drive them to action?

You could build relationships with other authors and people of influence who could help you spread the word about your book?

You had a core group of "super fans" that helped you make hard decisions about what to write next, including new ideas, genres, or markets?

You knew that your next book would be a success, even before you started writing it?

This gives you a whole new level of confidence in your writing. It gives you the motivation to keep working and producing. Another great perk is, it provides personal fulfillment as you hear directly from your fans how your work is improving the quality of their lives, and you'll discover how to build lasting connections with an audience.

I created this course for any author who wants to be ahead of the curve for platform development.

It is also a bit of an ego rush to a degree, when it comes to seeing your name in print, especially when fans take pictures of your work on their shelves, or at a public place. I went to a library in a city I had never been to and saw a few copies, as well as at more than a few bookstores. It always makes me happy to know that I am appreciated. The feeling of satisfaction of seeing my bookshelf grow with my titles motivates me, it is also a legacy. My books are like my children, they are created, they grow, once published, and they will live long after me, keeping my name and ideas in circulation as they are continually printed or copies are handed down from one owner to the next.

I also hated being under someone's watchful eye. One of the great things about being self-employed is that there is no boss looking over your shoulder and telling you what to do. One of the tough things about being self-employed is that there is no boss looking over your shoulder, telling you what to do. That is why it is imperative that you are disciplined and self-motivated. You are the boss of you!

That brings me to my next topic: how to keep yourself focused on the task at hand.

How to get started, and the difficult part once you do, how to stay motivated.

We all have those days where we feel highly motivated and proud of our level of accomplishment. We feel as if we can take on anything. Unfortunately it seems for every day we have that we can rock out, there are ten times as many days where we feel unmotivated, and like it takes a Herculean effort just to get out of bed. Not everyone is a workaholic, which has just as many issues. Sometimes you just have to force yourself to get to work. Unlike other jobs where you punch a clock then go home and your time off is time off, as a writer, every moment you aren't doing something productive you are piling up life's debts. How, you might ask, do you get motivation when you feel sluggish? As I said before, I don't have all the answers, but I am happy to share what I do, in this case, rest assured there are useful techniques you can use get the most out of each day.

People are creatures of habit. In knowing that, you can form good habits, such as creating a routine. What I do first thing in the morning is get my caffeine in to jog my brain into function, as I am not really a morning person. I check my email in personal and business, to be responsible to colleagues and customers and keep a good reputation, a critical aspect of being in the public eye. Then I move onto my Facebook accounts, to do the same thing. I wouldn't honestly have them if I wasn't a writer because I am a shy introvert. I use them to keep people up to date with my appearances, my art, or what books will be coming out.

I paint and write best in the afternoons and at night. Because I have to deal with the business aspects, and then I can relax and I feel the flow of the creativity gets stopped by the daily grind. I believe parts of the brain handle tasks and critical thinking and other parts of the brain are responsible for being creative, so I think I have a pretty good rhythm down. I know for other writers, it's different. I know more writers work through the night but there are some who are used to office work that become authors that stick to the biorhythm they are used to, like getting up early to work. In my case, if not interrupted, I'll work on an average of ten to thirteen hours a day with the occasional stretch and restroom break. My friends and fans even stop me at events and ask me if I have eaten for the day because I tend to forget to take care of myself. I do know that proper sleep and diet is important, because your brain will function better when you do so I do force myself, by an alarm or sticky notes as a reminder, to eat more than once a day.

Like most people we have things we don't want to do but need to anyway. It is human nature to put off things we do not like to do, and we will find all kinds of ways to avoid working. Procrastinating was something I used to do in school, until I started college. I think what changed is the fact I knew I was paying for college and wanted to get my money's worth. I went from a C average high school student to fifteen years later in life as an honor student. Life sometimes changes people due to perspective, so you can break negative habits.

Sometimes we need to reward ourselves for reaching a goal, but I try to keep it realistic and push regardless of treating myself because the items marked off my long list is a reward to me, the feeling you get when you actually finish a task. For each person it is different.

Most people find it difficult to keep working on your own every day due to being lonely, they need someone else around. Feedback and hearing another's perspective can indeed help. I know I enjoy a weekend off or even one day every two weeks to get away to the movies or shooting. I find it fun and stress relieving. Another thing about being around your friends is that if you share your goals with people it may even force you to make more of an effort to actually do them.

Most new authors do nothing but promote their new title, which you do need to do, but what will sell the most copies is simple. Just write more books. Nothing sells your older books like writing new ones! Many successful authors (both indie ones and self-published) turn out a lot of books. This will help you gain a following. In doing so, you bring new readers to both books; old fans read the new ones, and new readers will keep buying your original titles, which creates a ripple effect that grows larger. That is why I have so many titles out. That and I cannot seem to shut my inner muse off no matter how exhausting it is to write nonstop for a living!

I get a lot done, yet it always seems as if I am weeks behind on the various projects I want to see happening. If you have ever stopped to think, there are never enough hours in the day to get it all done, I totally understand. You cannot let it defeat you, however. By saying it is too much, we give up on what could be out of despair. Instead, dedicate segments of your day, every day, to get certain things done.

There is no such thing as luck. The opportunities we get we determine for ourselves. Someone once told me I was lucky because things just seemed to happen for me. That couldn't be further from the truth. I worked for years proving myself until others took notice. People know people and I was introduced to other like-minded folks who achieved big themselves and fancied me as cut from the same cloth as they were. You see, when someone takes a chance on you, they put their own reputation on the line, so do your damnedest to prove you are worth it. IF you do well, it not only impresses those who are added to your Rolodex, but the mentor is proud and helps you again. THEY feel proud about your triumph and it adds a feather in their cap. We'll cover this deeper later on in the course when we get to reputation.

The average American watches thousands of hours of television before even entering school, and unfortunately, it isn't learning programs, like Sesame Street, these days. Laziness is the source of any low achievement, and it beats a low IQ. The vast majority, at best, live as poet Henry David Thoreau put it, "...lives of quiet desperation and go to the grave with the song still in them." In more common vernacular, as my friend, Brooke, once told me, "Most people are just dead inside. So depressing and boring when people are not motivated."

## Beating Procrastination

Procrastination is death to those who want to get ahead, it wastes your time. Quitters will throw in the towel whenever difficult tasks are thrust before them, but those bent on success will overcome the challenges life offers, seeing it as a fight to charge in on and beat it, with confidence.

Look at where your time goes. Remember what I said a little bit ago about watching television instead of reading a book? This is also an indication you waste your time. We all use different props to fill our time when we're procrastinating, so try to identify what these are for you. Do you fill your time browsing social media, play games, or scour the internet for random gossip links? We need to consciously resist these things, it all adds up to what could have been. In my case, a new book being written, which has a ripple effect of bills not getting paid, of fans not getting the information I researched faster, and it goes on. Understand that NOT getting your goals met has consequences just as surely as there are consequences for maximizing your time. See, that pesky thing called choice rears its head again. It can be all too easy to click on a digital device when a task is too boring or difficult to do. In college, we had a class on becoming a better student and at the start of the class they had us keep a chart for a week, making a note of exactly where your time goes. Most people rack up time as watching television or doing errands, taking care of children, class, etc. some of which you cannot avoid; we must be responsible adults after all and unwinding from a hard day by entertaining ourselves is important to reduce stress.

Try it yourself, you will be shocked by how many hours are spent non-productively. Procrastinators frequently delude themselves regarding the passage of time. If you often tend to get to the end of the day bewildered as to where the day went, this technique will make you become aware of exactly what you could do instead.

I know I write four to ten hours a day and get six books out, sometimes as many as eight per year. Of course, some days are spent doing radio interviews, signings at stores and conventions, as well as the time to travel to these locations, but that is all time well spent. I will listen to motivational videos on YouTube, read a book, prep my speaking notes or re-read my own books in order to be more fluid when giving a presentation. All this builds confidence so people think I just know my material. Well, to a degree, I do, but with so many titles I have written, even I need a refresher on the content because I get asked to do talks on topics written years ago.

We tend to procrastinate most when the task we're facing is at either end of the scale. If it is too easy we get bored and have little motivation. I know, painting landscapes, for me, is incredibly easy and I make good money at it but don't do them often because I am not challenged. But who am I hurting? Me, financially because not only is the 'easy' money lost to me, and also I hurt my fans who could own or gift something they want to purchase. Someone pointed out to me, despite the fact I love to paint a variety of content, my erotica pieces are not 'family' safe and only a few collectors will buy them because they can't hang them in their living rooms even if they like my posts on my art page on social media!

If the task is too difficult, we tend procrastinate even more often. The reasons here are different, obviously. We know the job ahead of us takes effort, we're perhaps not sure whether we can do it, scared, or let's be totally honest, too lazy to do it. We put it off and put it off, doing anything other than the thing that needs to be done. Finally, it gets done but usually at the cost of flaws that could have been caught if we had more time to double check our work. If we want to succeed, our reputation needs to be perfected, and only by repeatedly being known for putting out quality do you gain respect. Respect and reputation get you paid, keeps food in your stomach and a roof over your head. Quality over quantity, and goody for you if you can accomplish both. Trust me, it is hard but I learned that my reputation leads me to have others want to co-author books with me and so I have more output in the same span of time and both of us benefit from the added fan base being exposed to our efforts. See? The ripple effect that has more and more good out of it. Deadlines are one way to deal with this, but a less stressful solution is to tackle the task while there's still plenty of time. Some people do better with deadlines, as it pushes them to get things done finally, however, that is stressful, for me, but if it is a proven method that works for you, and you spent the other part of your time wisely doing other truly useful things, then good for you, use what works.

Of course, you can say there are only so many hours in a day. I work 100 hours a week, fifteen hours a day. True, I work from home and do not have to commute, which helps, but before I left my day job, I worked a full-time job, did housework, wrote several books a year, published as many as thirty others, and went to college where I received scholarships and academic awards for, not one, but two different degrees. You can always find people to help you. I know, control freaks have trouble with this suggestion. Instead of doing something you're not good at, you're better off hiring someone, or asking for a favor from a friend, who can fill in the skills you lack, either as a contractor as needed or full-time tech or personal assistant. Besides compensating for your weakness, this will help empower the people who work for you if you own your own business.

You see, you need to have the will of a fighter, a sense of competition. I have found that in life if you have someone to compete with (real or even imaginary) it pushes you to do better, do things faster to get the prize. Especially when you compete with others, you may find the others

24

have the better methods in how they go about it and you can discover new ways to get ahead. There is no shame in going by other's examples if it works. Remember, everyone needs to grow and think outside of the box. Otto von Bismarck wrote, "A fool learns from his mistakes, but a truly wise man learns from the mistakes of others." He was German Chancellor from 1862 to 1890.

I asked my friend, Robert Ing, how he would suggest anyone seeking to advance themselves in a business move beyond those around them, to stand out in the same profession? His response was deep but easy to grasp.

"Today, especially in most professions, a professional will offer the exact same services their peers do. The only way to advance is differentiation. That differentiation and competitive edge is the individual themselves. There is a saying, 'it's not what you do but how you do it.' As a professional in private practice for three decades, I successfully stood out because people remembered and enjoyed the persona I conveyed in doing my job. Taking an interest in them, being relatable to aspects of their own personality and just being approachable all helped in making their experience and selection of my services all the more easier for them. I would also strongly advise people to write articles, write a book, build connections to local media (radio, tv, print) as being the 'specialist', do some volunteer work on a regular basis and don't forget to get known at events in the local community. All these things will help you break down barriers and make you the 'go to' person in the community for the professional service you offer. This is all you, your personality. In doing this you put a living, breathing person and personality to your practice and you will be the person who gets the call. The professional world is both competitive and constantly changing so in order to be on top you must never stop being a student. That is, invest in taking at least a course or two a year, read trade magazines and new books that relate to your field, get a professional certification if there is one for what you do even if it is not mandatory. Professional development such as this is an investment that will see you advance in your career ahead of others and keep you relevant over the years in your field."

We never stop growing and learning, if we realize that, accepting our current lot in life is nothing less than stagnation. Stagnation and being in a rut can kill progress. You can enjoy the sweet victory of success but not for long. Never stay satisfied with the present achievement. You need to stay motivated to do it again, to see if you can push yourself more. Never bypass any opportunity that will push you to be better.

**Tricks to increase productivity**

Kevin Kruse's new book *15 Secrets Successful People Know About Time Management*, intrigued me. In it, he interviews seven billionaires, 13 Olympic athletes, and 239 entrepreneurs. The book was an easy read; it didn't disappoint.

What stood out to me, in particular, were these time-management tips from some of the most successful people on the planet.

Richard Branson, founder of the Virgin Group, says, "One of my favorite tricks is to conduct most of my meetings standing up. I find it to be a much quicker way of getting down to business, making a decision, and sealing the deal. When given the opportunity, I often like to take things a step further--literally, with a walking meeting. I think the number one thing that I take with me when I'm traveling is the notebook... I could never have built the Virgin Group into the size it is without those few bits of paper... If you have a thought but don't write it down, by the next morning it may be gone forever."

Deciding on what are truly your priorities is the first and the most important step. To stay on top of my busy life I make lists and start off with those in order of importance. At the end of your day, review what you've done and make a new list for the next day. In my follow through, I commit. I am pretty ruthless about setting priorities but you have to be sure it is really and truly a priority, you have to learn to differentiate between the important and the urgent. What's important is not always urgent. What's urgent is not always important. If a task takes less than five minutes, do it right away, get it off your mind. Deal with e-mail at set times each day, instead of checking it constantly – unless you know something really important is expected which you know you have to take care of immediately.

You have got to eliminate the time wasting that always happens. If you know that phone calls are taking up too much time, you obviously have the ability to turn off your phone for as long as you need. That's what voicemail is for!

Learn to value your time. Most people don't value your time, they value what they can get from you, and will slow your productivity down if you let them. Set boundaries.

Use your down time (e.g., waiting for meetings to begin) to, for example, update your to-do list or return calls.

Don't procrastinate, get projects done early. It takes them off your mind, I did this all through college and then used my free time to write books. I did that while working third shift at hotels because I still got paid to work but in downtime, earned my future at the same time, making the best use of what was free.

Try to get it right the first time. Going back to repeat your work causes stress and wastes time. It usually takes a lot more time to fix something.

Some people advise that you stop multitasking. Why? When you try to do many things at the same time, it is hard to focus and get everything right. Conversely, it also helps, when you get stuck on one project because writer's block, to jump over to another book for a while. That is one of my secrets in knocking out six to eight books in one year!

If the opportunity cost is too high, say no. Learn to say no, another section in this course will add clarity, but I do not want to be repetitive so let's move on. See? Time management!

If you can afford to pay someone to do something, do it. Time is your most valuable asset if you can pay money to save time...DO IT. I did that while writing this book by paying someone to transcribe an entire two hour lecture I had done with another speaker. Because of this, we were able to put out two titles at the same time. All I had to do was edit and add additional commentary, an introduction, afterword, and suggested reading, as did my co-author. I often put out a few books a year with co-authors because it saves me time, gets more titles out, yet it also has a surprise benefit of opening your eyes up to other perspectives.

It costs, yes, but delegating your work is smart, not lazy. Get interns, like I do with my business. The small things anyone can do for you saves you time to focus on what only you are able to do. It will give you more time to focus on the most important things. Hire experts, they took the time to learn specifics, it isn't your job to know it all. Smart and successful people surround themselves with skilled people.

Make the most of every day. If you aren't interested in waking up trying to make a better living or enjoying yourself more, then I have no idea why you want to take this course!

You will discover many of the lessons learned here overlap and make use of other sections, which is the theory of putting it all together. Remember the words of Aristotle "We are what we repeatedly do. Excellence, then, is not an act, but a habit." Just don't make it that way in everything you put your name on because it spreads your "self-made" reputation out to be just a networker and partner. Use moderation, another form of common sense practicality.

Value your time and other people will do the same. Mark Cuban, owner of the Dallas Mavericks, Magnolia Pictures, and Landmark Theatres says, "Never do meetings unless someone is writing a check." Time is a limited aspect of our lives, and you need to get the most out of every day you live. Time really is money. It's a matter of doing the right thing at the right time. The reason is simple - there is always an opportunity cost for the things that you didn't do. In business and life, we're facing this situation and problem very often. Here are some techniques to do that, which I wasn't able to share prior to this edition:

In most cases, distractions are much more tempting than doing the right things. Get into the habit of switching off email whenever you can, even if this is only for 15 minutes or 30 minutes at a time. This goes for social media also. There was a meme I saw that said as a writer I spend "x" amount of time checking email, social media, researching, and the thinnest part of the pie chart was actual writing. That is because we tend to avoid the actual 'work' then complain that we are not able to find the time!

## Setting goals

When our goals seem too big, it can feel impossible, so break it down into smaller subsections. By seeing the goal as less massive, you can keep yourself motivated and take it on as one small part after another and build momentum. Stop looking for a way out by saying it cannot be done.

You can also work on developing this as an attitude like some people do with a mantra. Every day when you wake up, affirm your achievable goals verbally aloud to yourself so that it matches your positive expectations. Sounds crazy but may help!

## Organization

Make a list, get organized. Check things off as you do them, trust me you will feel accomplished and it exponentially increases your productivity. I am OCD, everything in its place. As busy as I am, I simply don't have the time to waste searching my office for interview dates, someone's address, or research materials.

Some other tips I have learned along the way. Set your priorities. The highest priorities for a writer who wants to make a living, are the things that earn your living, so focus on your most important tasks that must be done and when. Schedule them and do them.

Delegate if at all possible. Get an assistant, or contact a college and get interns who can help. Not only does this help you in getting more of your work done, it also gives someone else job experience to add to their resume.

Focus on critical things with zero distractions; no phone calls, don't have the email account up, and turn off all social media. I amazed myself and did this entire section in a week (adding this comment in while doing final edits).

*Overworking and feeling overwhelmed*

Two extremes of behavior seem to be the given for writers I know. Either we overwork ourselves into the ground, or we feel overwhelmed by the weight of all the requirements that exist in being in the profession we have chosen. I tend to fit into the overworked part myself; it seems as if I fill every moment with new projects, events, or radio interviews in fear of being forgotten about. In my defense, it is a valid concern, as the general public does have a short attention span. However, when my roommates point out in 2014 that they found me asleep at my computer more than three times I do realize I take it a bit too far. Hence my stressing the advice of authors, or any self-employed business owner, to come up with a schedule and stick to it as best you can.

Is feeling overwhelmed stopping you from what you want to do, or really should be doing? Too often, people use overwhelm as the excuse not to do something. They don't have time, they don't know where to start, and they are just...overwhelmed. I have a lot of personal experience with this one. Get rid of clutter and get your home and life in order.

I get a lot of questions from radio hosts, usually on the topics of my books, but the one that keeps coming up is, how do you stay focused and get so much done? Well, to be truthful, I struggle with time management but am getting better at it. I understand that clearing out 20 years of accumulated crap is not something any of us would look forward to doing; however, it can and has to be done.

# Traditional vs Small Press vs Self-Publishing

Before I get into the lengthy explanation of how to get published by a big company, and have a lot of work taken off you, as well as tell you what I discovered about putting out books through someone like Schiffer Books, I feel it only fair to cover the pros and cons of each type of publishing, in depth, so that you can decide which one to pick, or, if you are like me, make the best use of all of them!

In the old days your only choice for being published was to have your work sent in to an agent, or, if you were lucky, directly to a publisher where the acquisition editor added it to a pile with hundreds of other hopeful writers whose work typically received a polite form rejection letter.

Publishing has changed with technology and those who fail to adapt suffer. Big business, big publishing houses, may make more money but are feeling the effects quickly too. Author friends of mine, that are published through the biggest companies, are sagging under the weight of warehouses of product, while the competition, with smaller and leaner methods of operation that take a personal approach instead, are holding their own, even in a bad economy. Like everything, there are good and bad aspects to deciding which way to go in being put into print. I have done both and will explain how each works and what I gained from it.

Let's start with old school, and how it has changed, as you need to know everything traditionally before you throw yourself headlong into do it yourself and have a travesty on your hands. Traditional bulk printings in comparison to the short turnaround of on demand or small runs.

## Traditional Publishing

The upside to traditional publishing is you will not have to worry so much about editing (but you have to send in a copy that has been proof read, not once, but several times by others!) and cover design is not your concern. Admittedly I have seen a lot of covers, on both self-published and traditionally published, that made me cringe, but my covers through Schiffer Publishing have all been great. Traditional publishers can also order books to be printed overseas, in large bulk orders, for a small cost per unit and so are able to afford large quantities at a time.

Going the traditional publishing route usually is a long process even if your manuscript does meet the submission standards of whatever publishing company you decide to go through. Be sure to read the submission requirements on the website of each publisher and get a copy of The Writers Market book for a resource list of the top companies all the way down to small press companies. It is a great tool to help you narrow down the genre. It lists the addresses and current editors. The worst thing in the world is to address the wrong person in a query letter. It shows a lack of diligent homework and is disrespectful. Get started on the right foot.

What is traditional publishing or trade publishing?

Traditional publishing refers to the deeply entrenched and established system of getting a book deal, which involves submission, usually to agents, over a very long and frustrating period of time, and hundreds of rejections until, finally, hopefully, your work is accepted. The agent will then submit the manuscript to publishers and, if the publisher accepts the submission, you get a contract and the agent collects their 20%. The book will then go through more edits, a cover design, pre-marketing, and will eventually be published.

*The pros of traditional publishing*
Some of the reasons you might choose this route are prestige of not

being self-published, awards and accolades, and the mental validation. Most authors suffer from self-doubt and wonder if their work is good enough, and if you always self-publish, you may always wonder if you could measure up with other established writers. I know I had that misgiving, after self-publishing six books, until Schiffer picked me up. If you make it through the process to get an agent, (we'll get into if you need one or not later) and then a publisher, this seems to make most authors reassured. If your definition of success includes a traditional mass market, despite if it sells well or not, then by all means take that road and don't look back. I'm not knocking those who do, but be aware it is most important that you are satisfied that you did your very best in writing your work (and fans love it) rather than basing your worth on who put you out, to be honest.

There are valid reasons as to why you may want to go this route, outside of the mental reassurances, especially for a new person. Print distribution in bookstores is far easier for a traditional publisher. They excel at moving massive amounts of books through sales channels that they have developed by creating relationships with the major book retailers such as Barnes and Noble. These book retailers have positions, called "buyers", which purchase quantities of books from sales representatives. Books are usually in the store for one to three months and only remain if they are hot sellers, because it is a heavy market that has a million titles being put out a year from every publisher and every author fighting for space.

Traditional publishing houses have very skilled professional teams in various departments to work with. If you do it yourself, you will either be forced to learn all of these technical skills or you'll need to have the money to hire someone who already has those skills. Reputable editors and graphics people, for cover designs, are not cheap nor easy to locate. Even less easy to find are the exact methods for formatting a book properly though there are some industry standards.

Marketing effort is usually related to how much is invested in the project. If you are already a famous author then the publisher is going to put more into getting the word out about your new book whereas, if you are not a known name yet, you will need to do most of your own marketing. Marketing for publishing companies is usually to book retailers, rather than consumers at large, because they know once books hit the shelf, it is up to the stores to move the product, and the authors to push their work. Surprised? I quickly discovered that, although being published by a much larger publishing company, most of my sales came from the same ways as I have been doing since I self-published my first book. Sadly, I received less per copy from sales than when I publish it through my own company. As rough as this sounds, I am only trying to establish the reality of the pros and cons of what happens to authors who have written for all three types of publishing. Many authors say they "only want to write," which is why they want a publisher to handle the rest of it, and are happy with spending the year to three, that comes between a book's completion and the printing, to market themselves and follow the rest of the advice I provide here in later sections.

There are other perks to this method to take into count, such as no upfront financial costs, which you will have if self-publishing, and there's sometimes an advance against royalties. You don't have to pay anyone to get a traditional publishing deal and if you are asked for money, then it is NOT a traditional book publishing deal. It's likely to be a vanity publisher and you should be very careful. A vanity, or subsidy, publisher charges a fee to produce a book, or requires the author to buy something as a condition of the publication of their book. With these type of publishing companies, they provide editing and cover design, as well as the opportunity for major distribution. You might be thinking "Great! Where do I sign up?" The problem with this is what comes next. These publishers then assign your book an ISBN number that belongs to them, often purchased in bulk, which makes them the publisher of record and entitles them to ownership of the book and royalties from sales of the book. These publishers also set the retail price of your book and so it might be higher or lower than you might like it to be.

The median author advance, from a traditional publisher, is currently around $10,000 USD. Increasingly, there are now deals where the author will take higher royalties and a smaller advance, or no advance at all. Remember, also, that the advance is against royalties, which are usually 7-20% of net book price. So if you get an advance of $10,000, you then have to earn more than $10,000 out of your royalty rate on book sales before you get any more money. If you don't sell enough to make that amount you may have to pay back some of that advance. I know several authors who fret over the fact they may or may not have to pay back advances, and even if their title has sold 6,000 copies quickly they feel panic. That may sound like a lot of books, and it is, but when a very large publisher takes a chance on you and says, here, take this six figure contract and three book deal but you better be able to help us sell 100,000 (or whatever amount) copies to your fans, well I know someone who is actually going through that right now.

Not all publishing contracts come with an advance. As a matter of fact, you probably won't get any advance from a large publishing company until you become a known name.

Critical acclaim, with literary prizes and other awards, are more likely through traditional publishing, and many literary prizes aren't even open to self-published authors. This may change over time, but thus far I haven't encountered it.

Potential to become a famous, well known author, like Stephen King, Dan Brown, J.K. Rowling, is more likely with a traditional publisher based on the ability to saturate the market. Below them are the second tier authors that people recognize, most of whom have been writing for many years, people like Dean Koontz and Nora Roberts, who are treated very well by traditional publishing and wouldn't see any reason to write for anyone else. Yes, there's a chance of becoming a writer of that notoriety by way of traditional publishing, but know that the odds are against you. It's very much like betting on the lottery. Think carefully about each method of publishing, and pick one that fits your mentality and personality.

*The cons of traditional publishing*
These are the issues with going the traditional route. Again, I'm not criticizing it, but everything has its advantages and disadvantages.

It is an incredibly slow process. By the time you have written your book, sent it to an agent (not to mention the time finding and being accepted by both an agent and a publisher) it may be a year at best or up to five years before they start printing your book. Writing and editing will be the same regardless of how you want to publish, no matter how you go about it, and then traditionally it takes from six months to two and half years before your book is launched. So it's a very, very slow process, which is crazy in this world of practically instant gratification.

Loss of creative control. You give this up when you sign with a publisher. Many authors get titles, covers, and marketing angles that they're not happy with. Sometimes you get an editor you don't agree with, and you are stuck with not only working with them, but they refuse to plead your case harder for adjustments on say, your font or color choice on the cover. I have noticed a lot of bad covers mixed in with great ones in several publishers' catalogs, and feel fortunate that five out of six of mine not only met my standards but surpassed expectations in the design. As a publisher and artist, I know what can help sell a book, but the difference between my company and larger publishers is that I know authors know best what they are trying to say with their work so it is best to get input from the writer while doing a cover. However, this rarely happens and the bigger the press, the less say you will get. The editor might also ask for changes within the book itself. They can ask you to change it completely or change the tone, or the wording, or any number of other things.

Low royalty rates. Royalty rates are a percentage of the profits from the sale of the book. They're likely to be net, so all the discounts, returns, marketing costs, and overhead costs are taken off the total before your percentage is calculated. Royalty rates for traditional publishing will usually range between 5% and 8%. The rates will also differ per format e.g. eBook vs. hardback vs. audio. Royalty reports may come every six months for a specific period of sales and many authors report how difficult they are to understand. I look at my statements from Schiffer every six months and see page after page of numbers and graphs of what sold versus what was returned and, although the transparency is great, they seem to me to be overly complicated. By the time you see the last page and compare what units sold of all titles in comparison to your end dollar amount, it is nowhere near what you dreamed of. I have a friend who writes for my company as well as a traditional publisher, and they tell me that, with 10% royalties from Dark Moon Press, they get paid more thru us because of the higher royalty rates. One of my friends barely earned $6.53 for one title selling for a six month period.

Lack of significant marketing help. Increasingly, authors have to do their own marketing and agents will often seek out authors who have a 'platform' or at least an email list of readers. If you do want a traditional publishing deal, make sure you ask them what is included for marketing and make sure you get more than just inclusion in a bookstore catalog.

Potentially prohibitive contract clauses.

This is worth its own section as there are a few issues that you need to watch out for.

One big issue is signing some contracts where they take World English rights in all formats. Don't do that, unless the money is really worth the risk. Your job and your agent's job, if you have one, is to keep as many rights as possible when you're doing a deal so you can exploit them in other ways, such as have the publisher do the US and Canada rights and then self-publish in the rest of the world. Be careful with formats as well, especially audio books. Many publishers take audio rights as part of a contract as well as electronic versions and only do paperbacks, keeping you from making other sales elsewhere on your own.

Once you sign a contract for your book, in their form it belongs to the publisher, and it may belong to the publisher for the life of copyright which is the life of the author as well as seventy years after your death. That is something to think long and hard about.

You have to really consider whether the money for the contract is worth it. This is where many authors think, "I should just take whatever contract I'm offered." Many authors will sign deals because they're grateful that they have been offered anything, but you need to value your work, and understand you have other options. Be sure to carefully read at the terms of the contract and the rights reversion clause. With things changing these days, with print-on-demand and eBooks, a book never has to go out of print. You have to consider when you might get your rights back, like in my case I decided to republish half of my works myself after discovering I retained the rights with the Library of Congress (I was listed as owner of content). So I changed my cover, reworded the title, and expanded the edition by adding a third more, thus printing a paperback, hardback, and eBook the way I really wanted it to be. Often your book will be edited down or they will ask you to remove large portions of your work because they either can't or won't print a larger page count due to costs.

If your publisher just isn't selling enough of your books and you think you can do a better job, learn from your experiences with the good and the bad, and maximize all of it when you set out to do it yourself.

Remember how important your rights are over the long term.

Publishers are not charities, they are a businesses and they want to make money. They are not doing you a favor by publishing your book, they judge if you are capable of making money for them, you simply get to be the one earning a living off of it. Traditional publishers take on the risk of publishing you by putting forth the money to print your book and hope that it sells. They *invest* in you and your work.

If you're looking at a traditional publishing, there are a couple of books I recommend reading to weigh your options even more:

*Deal Breakers: Contract Terms Writers Should Avoid* by Kristine Katherine Rusch

*The Self-Publisher's Legal Handbook* by Helen Sedwick

*How Authors Sell Publishing Rights* by Orna Ross and Helen Sedwick

These books will help you with contract terms, so do your homework and spend a little money to save yourself a lot later.

Most people will have a favorite book and they'll know the name of the author, but, often, they don't know or care about the name of the publisher. Of course, having said that, pick who you go to as your publisher by carefully reading their website, talk to others who writ for them via social media, or whatever way they are likely to respond, and find out how they get treated (sometimes you can get them to divulge much more if they truly are dissatisfied), and you especially need to go over your contract with a fine toothed comb.

So your publishing choice is more a question of the outcome that you want to achieve and your personal definition of success rather than who does it for you.

Would I take a traditional publishing deal again? Absolutely. For the right project and for the right terms, conditions, and potential reach they have, of course, that would help sell other books I have. If they got my name out there more and it helped my back catalog of thirty some titles sell exponentially then I would do it.

I choose to get my books out into readers' hands as soon as possible and take the cash sooner rather than waiting years to months on small royalties. I have my validation from having been accepted several times by a more known publisher so that is no longer a question, and I see my Amazon reviews are as good on both traditional and self-published books so I know my fans will follow me no matter how I choose to print my work. I'm primarily an indie author and publisher, so let's now look at the pros and cons of small press, the in between, the best of both worlds, and finally we will compare it to self-publishing.

The process of submitting to publishers is usually explained on each publisher's website so follow their instructions. Completely. If you don't, it ends up in the trash.

*The Pros and Cons of Publishing with a Small Publisher*
"As the editor of Writer's Market, I'm often quizzed by writers about which is the better option: self-publishing, or getting an agent and trying to land a deal with a big book publisher," says Robert Lee Brewer.

"While many professionals seem to acknowledge only these two paths to publication as well, there's a third route that should not be overlooked: the small press. There's a whole field of reputable publishers outside of New York's 'Big Five' that can offer the support of the traditional publishing model on a smaller scale—and most accept unagented submissions."

Let's examine the usual steps to small press, starting with submitting your material.

*The Submissions Process*
There are some crucial differences in what small press editors look for in a submission, in contrast to the larger companies. When I speak with other writers at conventions they often voice frustration over the importance of writing commercially marketable stories while sacrificing the 'pushing the creative envelope' and the lack of true risk-taking in the business. Authors are less business people and get into it to release their creativity and fantasies into the world, and big publishers are like television content editors (as I discovered when doing a television pilot to pitch, it is a lot alike). People in big mass media service of all types only keep their eye on the big trendy types of books, shows, and music that is a huge hit right this second and rarely take chances on new material. That's what we keep hearing, subtly or directly, emphasized by editors because those professionals have aggressive sales goals. Small presses do as well, but they're typically

more willing to take risks on projects they believe have artistic merit. Small presses, like mine, are created typically by creators who dream of putting out artistic masterpieces and yet try to have the accumulation of sales that the big boys have also. Making big money off risky edgy material may be hard to do, but worth the struggle to retain integrity as a creative person.

Jen Michalski, who in 2013 published a novel, a novella, and a short-story collection says, "The most important draw about these presses was their willingness to publish work that was risky, a difficult read, and therefore inherently commercially unsuccessful."

Smaller presses view publishing and sales differently because they have less overhead, less stock to move, and can take more risks with less inventory to lose. "With a small press, there is no 90-day window to make your book a bestseller," Press 53 Publisher Kevin Morgan Watson says. "We continue to market and support our books and authors years after the book is released. It's a marathon, not a sprint."

If you think a small press might be a good fit for your work, what should you know about your options? Whether the books are made available as print, digital, or both, know that authors earn their money primarily through direct sales of their copies. That is, they buy their own books from the publisher at half price of the cover, usually, and then resell them. Royalties are not usually what gets you the majority of your earnings. On average, advances, if there are any, tend to be small, from a few hundred to $1,000, or usually nonexistent because a small press doesn't have enough sales of all books, in volume, to warrant it, let alone enough powerhouse seller titles, to make it worth the risk.

Of course, how many copies you can expect to sell will depend on your book, as well as the distribution and fan base you personally can build.

Many small presses solicit manuscripts by way of open submission periods and book contests.

*The Publishing Process*

Small press authors can expect to receive a lot of attention from the editor and owner. That can translate into a better writer-company relationship, as well as more involvement with the sales and promotion, after all, you both have a lot on the line.

"We take the time to make sustaining connections for authors in the world of literature, scheduling author tours and creating a thoughtful list of prizes to nominate their work," says Megan Bowden, director of operations and outreach for Sarabande Books.

In my case, I discuss distribution and marketing ideas with my authors, and ask them what they see as a cover concept for the suggested design.

"I work directly on each book, designing it along with the author, to produce something that a reader will want to purchase, as well as an object that best fits how the author wants their writings to be displayed," says Geoffrey Gatza, founder, editor and publisher of BlazeVOX [books].

Of course, while book design and editorial input are important for any author, that doesn't mean you should expect complete creative control over the final outcome of the book when you open that long awaited case of books. If you demand that level of control, then your best option is learn how to do it all and self-publish.

Small presses are also a business. They try to do what's best for the author and the sales of the book. Small press owners will hear the desires of the author, but with experience the writer doesn't have, so that, when an author agrees to publish their work with a small press, they trust that the company they picked is truly going to work hard and do all that we can to create a cover that works with the overall theme of the book. Unlike the writer, who is usually new to the industry, they understand the retail side of the publishing world enough to know how a book should look and feel to the reader.

Small presses offer unknown and emerging authors a start in their pursuit of success by publishing their early works upon which a career is started, this helps them get a name without having to learn all of the parts of self-publishing.

"The advantage of being a published author is what most of us want, and a small press can do that tremendously well," Gatza says. "A small press is the stepping-stone to bigger and better things, and not an end for a book—it is a wondrous beginning."

Unlike with self-publishing, this beginning is endorsed by someone who believes in your work enough to invest time, energy, and money in the book and pay you for the effort, usually more, per sale than larger companies will, and usually market you more.

Of course, small press authors are expected to do their part as well.

"We expect our authors to be actively publishing nationally and promoting through local and regional events and activities," Watson says. "You can't sit back and wait for readers to find you. Creativity does not end with writing the book."

I agree. With Dark Moon Press I always explain to new authors that they can't expect a book to sell itself just because it is on Amazon, B&N.com, and the shops I have accounts with, they have to get out there and meet fans at events and beat the streets. Even larger publishers won't actively market you unless you are one of the top dog earners. That is the way of the publishing business.

Now let's look at the other methods of publishing a book, self-publishing.

## Self-Publishing: Full Control, Full Responsibility

The pros of being an indie author are pretty nice. You get total creative control over content and design. As I mentioned previously, many authors who were in traditional publishing and are now in self-publishing talk about how painful it was to have a cover or title they hated, or to have editorial choices imposed on them that they didn't agree with but had to live with it.

I hear the complaints about publishers all the time, from new aspiring writers to people who have been at it forever. No or little cover input, little for royalties, pressured to dumb down their work, lack of help in promotion and contacts shared.

Author Kristen Lamb writes a blog on helping authors, and her opinion on independent or self-publishing does not carry the stigma it once had. "When I began writing I was SO SURE agents would be fighting over my manuscript. Yeah. But after almost fourteen years in the industry, a lot of bloody noses, and even more lessons in humility, I hope that these tips will help you. Self-publishing is AWESOME, and it's a better fit for certain personalities and even content (um, social media?), but we must be educated before we publish. In fact, my last book Rise of the Machines is much more than a social media book. I dedicate a large portion of the book to explaining how the various forms of publishing work, because you need to make the best choice for YOU.

The problem with the ease of self-publishing is that it is, well, too easy. Just because anyone can self-publish, doesn't mean they should. A lot of writers rush into self-publishing without properly preparing to be a small business, yet that is exactly what we are. When we self-publish, we take on a ton of new roles and we need to understand them, and all the steps involved. I learned little by little by mentors, books, online articles, and trial and error. We need to be willing to fork out money for proper editing, cover design and formatting."

One of the benefits to traditional and/or small press publishing is that they take on all the risk and do the editing, proofing, etc. When we go it alone, we need to prepare for some expenses and do our research.

I went to college for business management and have my taxes done for me. It isn't a decision to be taken lightly. There are a lot of writers who mistakenly believe that self-publishing is a fast track to fame and success. Wake up and get ready for a mountain of work.

Having said that, the myth of traditional publishing doing all the work to get you out there is not happening. Unless your name is Stephen King, J.K. Rowling, or Laurel K. Hamilton, forget about up front royalties and huge paydays, a best seller is not a first time author's reality.

There are many reasons self-publishing isn't for everyone. Authors need to keep at it, in marketing and connecting with fans, and stop relying on their publisher to make them a millionaire. We need to write prolifically and keep ourselves in the public eye at conventions or anywhere that will let us get copies into the hands of the public. We need to get attention on social media. Ask yourself, how badly do you want the dream, and then ask how many hours are you willing to work? This is true for whatever way your book(s) become published.

In traditional publishing, this takes time because we are dealing with a publisher's schedule. Most of my books through Schiffer took a year or two before they went from submission to printed copy. In self-publishing, we can make our own schedule, but it requires hard work in either case. The major difference is higher payments per copy, total control over content, and to be able to put out as many books as quick as you can write them.

As an indie, you can work with freelancers of your choice and you can choose the ultimate look and feel of your product. Now, that can be a pro or a con depending on how the book ends up, but as an indie, you can also change it by just uploading a new file.

Empowerment for more and more people is a factor here. The Journal of Personality and Social Psychology reported that the number one contributor to happiness is autonomy, "the feeling that your life – its activities and habits – are under your control." After signing a contract, traditionally published authors have pretty much zero control – over pricing, timing of publication, marketing, the cover, the title, and even the words themselves. Plenty of authors are told to change their stories to fit what a publisher wants. Compare that to the empowerment of the indie author who can learn new skills, work with professionals, make mistakes and learn from them, earn money directly, and interact with customers. Yes, it's hard work, but it's certainly empowering. The positive energy involved in being an indie can propel you much further, much faster, than waiting in line for your turn.

Faster time to market. You still have to spend the same amount of time writing and editing. But once you're ready to publish, you upload your files to Amazon, Kobo, iBooks, Draft2Digital, Smashwords and any other stores. Your eBook is usually for sale within 4-72 hours. You're paid 30 to 60 days after the end of the month of sale. If you're doing print on demand, you can get that up within 24 hours if you approve the formatting online. Or, you can order a copy and it might take a couple of weeks, but essentially, it's incredibly quick to get your book up for sale. This certainly suits my personality, as once I'm done with a book, I want it out there and selling! I don't want to sit on it for several years while it shuttles around publishers.

Higher royalties. If you price your book between $2.99 and $9.99 (on Amazon), you can get a 70% royalty. Traditional royalty rates usually fit in the 5-10% bracket, averaging 7%. It's clear that you need to sell far fewer books in order to make the same amount of money with self-publishing but it's not a get rich quick scheme. That's really important. You can't guarantee that you're going to make as many sales as you would've done with a traditional publisher, or indeed, any sales. That has more to do with genre, investment in marketing, and sometimes pure luck. An author can't build a business on luck – but they can learn about marketing, and authors have to do that these days, regardless of how they publish.

Sell by any means in any global market, as you retain the rights. My books have now sold in thirteen countries that I know of. Years ago, I was only selling books in the US, UK, Australia, Canada and now every month another income stream starts up as my printing company adds new countries. This is for books in English by the way – we're so lucky that English is the most international language. Many traditionally published authors have sold World English rights for all formats and yet have barely sold outside the usual country markets because their books aren't even available in most places in the world.

Use it to get into the game. These days, if you self-publish and do well, agents and publishers will come to you. For example, look at the incredible success of The Martian, which started off as a self-published eBook, then went into audio, and then became a movie and worldwide phenomenon. And let's not forget 50 Shades of Grey which started out as self-published fan-fiction before selling 65 million copies.

*The cons of being an indie author*
So there's the positive side, but what about the negatives? Remember, total responsibility!

You need to do it all yourself or find suitable professionals to help. As with any new skill, it's a steep learning curve. You still, obviously, have to do the writing and marketing, but you also have to do the publishing. You have to find an editor and a cover designer, and work with them, decide on the title, get your work formatted into eBook, print, and any other format you want and find suitable professionals to help. This isn't such a big deal as we all share with each other online and you can join The Alliance of Independent Authors. But you do have to decide on your definition of success and understand that you need to run all aspects of the business if you want to go the professional indie route. For many people, this is a negative, because they just don't have the time to do everything or they don't enjoy doing it. I'm lucky because I love being an entrepreneur. I love all aspects of what I do, from idea generation to writing, to making covers. After many years, I've found the perfect work for me. If you can manage a project or you could learn to, then you'll likely enjoy it too. But this life is certainly not for everyone.

There's no prestige, kudos, or validation by the industry. The 'stigma' lessens every day, but it still has some negative connotation, and largely because people put out badly formed books.

You need a budget upfront if you want a professional result. These days, you're likely to spend on professional editing before submitting to an agent anyway, or at least be spending on books and courses for writers. If you are like me, you're intending to make a living from this, then yes, you need to invest money in creating intellectual property assets for the business with the intention of getting it back through multiple streams of income.

It's difficult to get print distribution in bookstores. It's certainly not impossible and if you care about print distribution then look at the options with Ingram Spark. Also check out the Opening Up to Indie Authors campaign. But you're much more likely to get bookstore distribution with a traditional publisher, as that's essentially their business model and has been for a long time. They are experts at printing and distributing physical product. My personal choice is to use Print on Demand through Createspace, so my print books are available on pretty much all online bookstores.

Most literary prizes don't accept indie books and most literary critics for mainstream media won't review them. So if your definition of success is literary acclaim, you're probably better off going the traditional route.

*Editing*
No matter how you decide to put your books out, get an editor. In fact, get more than one, and of different types. I am not good with my first draft, my business partners in the past have trouble figuring out what I mean sometimes, calling it "Eric speak". I truly feel sorry for them and my first editor at Schiffer Publishing, Dinah Rosenberry! My mind works so very fast that I know what I am trying to say yet I did not do great at grammar in elementary school, despite having an extremely high IQ and reading nonstop. While I aced Literature and Philosophy

classes and am considered an expert on many subjects, I need a good proofreader to catch my sentence structure. Take heart, even well respected authors, from big publishers, will print books with mistakes, it happens, no one can catch everything. Just do your best, and get people like an English professor to red pen your work, then have a test audience to tell you what they think. I say that because your friends or family usually will tell you what they think you want to hear and you are not served well by being fed sugar coated lies that you are the new *New York Times* Best Seller.

*Formatting*

The biggest frustration in starting out as a self-published writer is in formatting. This is not an issue for me, as I simply haven used the same template and just changed the fonts on the headers and sub headers from book to book, same with the font of the title page (I always match it with the font of the cover). I also have hired someone to check the formatting on the books we publish.

Originally however, it can be tricky. Make sure to look at other publisher's guidelines to get an idea of how you might want to format your own.

*Cover design*

The old myth of don't judge a book by its cover is a flat out lie. As a publisher, and a buyer of books, I know full well customers only initial way to value a book immediately is to look at the cover (or an online thumbnail image) to see if they want to look into it more deeply.

"Much like an incredible cover image can be the decision between someone picking up your book or not, your author photo also gives potential readers a visual to attach to your book. If your author photo looks blurry and unprofessional, they might assume that the work inside was also left unpolished," says SparkPoint Studio's senior publicist Sara Chambers. As far as book cover formatting, if you're using Ingram you'll need a professional. Don't try this one yourself unless you're skilled with InDesign. If you're not, leave it to the professionals, hire it out.

Update Your Head Shot. Have at least one or three great headshots. Look at other author's books, blogs, and social media. A lot of them have a photo in an outdoor setting, or with a background that fits the style of the author's personality, again, consider your personal brand. A picture says a thousand words; it conveys who you are to your fans.

*Printing options*

There are a slew of options to get books made if you are serious about printing them yourself and have the dedication to learn how to do all of these steps. Let's examine the most common.

*Print on Demand*

Suggested POD (print on demand) resources and the advantages and disadvantages of them both. Ingram Spark, like Lightning Source (both of which are an Ingram company) launched its new self-pub platform. We'll cover all of those here.

I only know a couple authors that use both Ingram Spark and Lightning Source and they seem happy, as they get them into Ingram's catalog and store. An old coworker of mine at the Ingram warehouse has said he has seen more than a few of my books at his work and I never used Lightning Source so it doesn't harm you to shop around.

With my first book, I was not aware of print on demand because it was in its infancy, so when I decided to put *out Embracing the Darkness Understanding Dark Subcultures* I had no option but to pay over $3,000 for printing and shipping copies. You can still bulk print for best discounted prices of around $3 for a 300 page book, but consider the storage space needed.

Using POD now, from most sources, costs you only a third of what using a big publisher cost you to buy copies of your own book at around 60% of cover. In addition, you may recoup your investment faster. The added bonus is you have control and visibility of your sales.

*Createspace*

A company I use often is CreateSpace; Amazon's POD platform. It is great for most every author producing a mainstream paperback for many reasons.

CreateSpace has a very easy to use interface, it costs nothing upfront, and they have 24/7 customer service. One of its best aspects is its affiliation with Amazon which provides a 60% royalty of your book's list price, minus the printing cost.

I use CreateSpace, for the reasons previously mentioned, and despite the fact it does offer "expanded distribution" to bookstores at no cost, bookstore owners' often say they won't consider carrying these titles so that is a drawback. Many indie bookstores are upset with Amazon, as they consider Amazon the competition, and they won't carry any book printed on the CreateSpace label, which is bad for indie or small press authors.

Self-published authors have to think from a booksellers' point of view, and knowing that, I created Dark Moon Press in order to offer books, at wholesale, to many bookstores, both online and brick and mortar stores alike, at a good and fair price.

Overall, I'm quite happy with the platforms I use and how user-friendly they've made it for independent publishers. The finished product looks as high quality as any other book on the market out there. Ingram's royalties are comparable with CreateSpace's expanded distribution, and if you want to create a hardcover version, Ingram offers that option as well.

*Lulu*

For this section I copied a review and 'how to' from a website that laid everything out, and personally, I agree with his findings. I use Lulu for some books for two big reasons. One, they do a fantastic job on hardback books, and you can find coupon/discount codes to save on printing costs. Lulu carries a much higher cost, as a POD, than CreateSpace but they do give you the option of hardback and spiral bound printing. ISBN numbers are included in the cost and they get you listed in Books In Print. Books In Print is a database for publishers, retailers, and libraries around the world. Books In Print provides a valuable resource for retailers in the process of making purchases. They also guide you through the process and provide great support and customer service to help you.

There is something to be said about a company that just puts it all out there. Between all of their FAQs and their user community, it seemed hard to go wrong with them. The most important, however, is the price. Lulu is bare-bones: you get an ISBN and you get listed everywhere important.

*How does it work?*

Lulu lists out all the steps in their help section:

After entering in your author and title, it asks you to pick the size, binding, and color. The most common size to pick is at 6″ x 9″ perfect binding, and black and white. Perfect binding is your typical paperback binding.

Next you need to upload the file.

Upload your book file (text, no cover) and Lulu coverts it to a print-ready file. Next, they ask for your cover to be uploaded, then the pricing and description. At the end you get a submit button. Keep in mind, this submit button locks in your author and title but not your content and cover. Press the button and you get the message, "You're published!"

The work has only just begun.

Purchase Published by Lulu or Published by You service and receive an ISBN.

"Published by Lulu" ISBN's are assigned immediately.

"Published by You" ISBN's take up to 3 business days to be assigned. This is because extra information needs to be processed with the ISBN Agency.

Revise the book to contain the ISBN number in the copyright page and add a bar code to the back cover (for one-piece covers), otherwise it appears on the back automatically, like with CreateSpace, if you just upload the front and back image files.

We chose the one-piece cover (you design it from scratch as one big piece) so that's what I'll talk about.

I am not comfortable with Photoshop CS3, so I hire my graphic work to be done by a professional. You also need access to Adobe Acrobat to make the PDF file. There are free PDF making programs but Acrobat has all the document control you need (quality, size, etc). I also use Microsoft Publisher because you can save images you create as jpegs and PDF files.

What you need, in the end, is a very high-quality PDF file that conforms to the printing company's size requirements. Look to their Book Covers FAQ for information and you can find your size on the chart.

Use their spine width calculator to find how big your spine is based on the number of pages. You will need to know how many pages your final version will be. If you're one or two off, it won't make a big difference but, if you can, be exact.)

Make your new picture in Photoshop or whatever program you are using. Set your resolution to 300 dpi or higher (I used 600 and it looked perfectly clean) and enter in the dimensions (height is listed on the site, width includes the spine. For a 6×9 with 120 pages it was 9.25" (9" + bleed, as listed) by 12.52" (6" x 2 + 0.27" spine + bleed).

First thing, set guides to indicate the spine (for our 6×9, the vertical guides were set at 6.125" (back cover + 1/2 bleed) and 6.395" for the spine).

Remember that there will be about 0.125″ cut off from every edge. If you have a picture/pattern that goes to the edges, you're going to lose a bit.

Now, you'll need to add a space for the barcode and, if you want, the product number from Lulu just makes it easy for people to find, and necessary for books stores to scan.

Saving the file was bit difficult. Make sure that the final size is correct and the resolution is what you set in the beginning. I set everything to the highest quality settings (highest quality for JPEG, reduce images to 600 DPI).

When you read through your final PDF manuscript, pay very close attention to which side the page number shows up on. The first page in the PDF will be the absolute first page in the book. Look at that page and say out loud "right." The next page falls on the left.

Purchase a proof copy of the newest version of the book.

After receiving and carefully reviewing the book, either:

a. Approve the book on Lulu.

b. Deny the book and make changes.

If the book needs revisions, make them and upload this new manuscript.

The book is uploaded to the distribution center within 3-5 business days for "Published by Lulu" distribution or 2 to 3 weeks for "Published by You" distribution.

The printer reviews the book to ensure it is up to standards. This can take up to 2 weeks.

Once accepted for printing, it can take another 6 to 8 weeks before the book is available through online retailers.

If rejected for not meeting requirements, you will be notified via e-mail that the book must be revised. You must then go back and make your revisions and start the process again from there.

Once that is finished the book becomes available for listing with online booksellers.

Online booksellers like Amazon decide whether or not they would like to list the book. Once a month, online booksellers update their databases with new books. When they update, if the booksellers choose to list your book, you will see the book listed as "currently available." This can take 6-8 weeks.

Read all publishing/printing FAQs. Pretty much every question you could have is contained in there. Don't skip over this just because you think you know what you're doing.

*Lightning Source*
Lightning Source is a business unit of Ingram Content Group. The company is a printer and distributor of print-on-demand books, equal to CreateSpace, that operates out of Tennessee. Like Amazon's CreateSpace, Lightning Source has an eBook supply system that can serve up protected PDF copies of books from their library, through a vendor's site, if a publisher/author chooses to take advantage of it.

They also offer their eBook on demand service to publishers who have a suitable vendor website, and supply eBooks to their retail partners, such as Powells.com, EBookmall.com, Diesel-eBooks.com, Fictionwise.com, Booksonboard.com and eBooksAboutEverything.com.

*Publishing With Ingram*
With Lulu, you can have boxes full of books printed for yourself as well as being carried by Ingram. Ingram is the largest book distributor in the world with a very good reputation that will broaden your exposure as an author (take a look at the Global Reach section of their website to view the list of distribution partners). If you want, your print-on-demand book will be included in the Ingram Content database. This gives you an edge over self-published authors who publish only with companies like CreateSpace.

So let's take a brief look at what it looks like to publish with Ingram, or as they list it specifically, Ingram Spark. First, you need to set up an account at www.ingramspark.com.

You must do a separate ISBN (if you have already gone through another company such as CreateSpace) and get a new one for your Ingram-distributed paperback so that you can keep track of sales through Ingram vs. Amazon (this also avoids confusion when Ingram submits your title to Amazon, which happens automatically. You want your CreateSpace version to be listed on Amazon for higher royalties, and if you have a separate ISBN, the CreateSpace book will supersede the Ingram Spark one, as long as it's been published first).

Create your cover file with the specific Ingram Spark template (which is very close to the CreateSpace specs, but must be made with the Ingram Spark template); your interior files will be identical, except for your ISBN on the copyright page.

Set up your title in the user-friendly interface, upload your files according to their guidelines (you can download this PDF from the Help section of the site), and pay the $49 setup fee, plus $12 for database inclusion.

Make any adjustments necessary to comply with guidelines OR pay a $10 fee to have Ingram fix error messages for you if you receive them.

Review your e-proof online when it's ready.

Make any necessary changes, re-upload your files, and repeat the online review process.

You can then order a printed proof, if desired or, if you've already completed that with your CreateSpace version, approve your title for distribution.

If you receive error messages when you upload, you can fix or bypass these errors to get to an e-proof stage by paying the $10 fee to have so-called errors corrected by the Ingram tech team (which, though not ideal, ends up being quicker and easier for the time being than fighting it), and they now have a customer support staff available Monday through Friday, 8:00–5:00 central time, at 1-855-99-SPARK.

If you want to be featured in the Ingram catalog that's sent out monthly to over 4,000 bookstores and libraries, you can, for a $60 fee. This gets you a one-time-only ad space in your genre with black and white cover image, description, and traditional book details. You can get your book in front of buyers, and while I have not done it myself, it might well be worth it as it is a small investment for the possibility of bookstore and library inclusion across the country.

## EBooks

Both Kindle Direct Publishing (KDP) and Smashwords offer distribution to other retailers and online library venues like Overdrive and Baker & Taylor (all other eBook formats) as well as a presales feature on their sites. So you can list your work for presales three months ahead of the print version.

*Kindle*

Kindle Direct Publishing for Amazon distribution (Kindle eBook) is another feature you can use with Amazon CreateSpace. I get about a quarter of all my book sales online from this, some authors sell thousands this way alone. Electronic books are here to stay regardless if old fashioned people, like me, love the feel and texture of a real, solid book in one's hands. Jeff Bercovici, Forbes Staff writer, says, "$5.25 billion: Amazon's current annual revenue from book sales, according to one of Packer's sources. That means books account for 7% of the company's $75 billion in total yearly revenue. 19.5%: The proportion of all books sold in the U.S. that are Kindle titles. E-books now make up around 30% of all book sales, and Amazon has a 65% and Barnes & Noble taking most of the remaining percent. The decrease in the number of independent bookstores over the past 20 years. There used to be about 4,000 in the U.S.; now there are fewer than 2,000. Amazon's arrival on the scene is only part of the story here, of course; the decline of the indies started with the debut of big-box stores like B&N.com and

Borders, which, by the end of 2009, all of Borders directly owned overseas locations had been sold or closed, with less than 10% of books are now sold through independent bookstores."

*Smashwords*
The founder of the company says, "Smashwords is the world's largest distributor of indie eBooks. We make it fast, free, and easy for any author or publisher, anywhere in the world, to publish and distribute eBooks to the major retailers."

For authors, publishers, and literary agents, Smashwords offers quick and easy eBook distribution to most of the world's largest eBook retailers. They provide free tools for marketing, distribution, metadata management, and sales reporting. At Smashwords, both authors and publishers have complete control over the sampling, pricing, and marketing of their written works. Smashwords is ideal for publishing novels, short fiction, poetry, personal memoirs, monographs, non-fiction, research reports, essays, or other written forms that haven't even been invented yet.

It is a difficult learning curve to upload files to Smashwords, so go over their website and look at reviews online for help.

On top of that, you will spend hours learning how to use Sigil to edit EPUB files. A tip on Smashwords from an online blogger, "If you use Smashwords Direct to upload a new EPUB, it will not replace the other file formats for your book. You need to upload your updated Word file (not docx but the 97-2003 version). My Advice: Use Mark Coker's template. If not, you're in for a very unwelcome surprise if you try to save your docx as its backward compatible cousin. JUNK lies hidden throughout your formatting that you won't see until it makes it through Meatgrinder and ends up in your sample download files."

All you need to do next is save the file, then also save it again but pick 'Save As PDF', which is what the printer will need in order to print your book. With all things, practice makes perfect.

Sometimes, it does depend on which PDF program you have; it gets tricky. If you are doing this yourself and converting directly from MS Word, you'll need Adobe Acrobat Pro XI to save in the proper format PDF/X-1a:2001 so the fonts are embedded and not saved as images.

## Making Good Use of all Three Methods
The hybrid model: It's not an either/or choice anymore.

The industry has changed and many authors now take a hybrid approach to publishing. They will make the decision by book and by particular rights, using the indie model for some things and taking traditional deals for others. This empowers the author to make decisions and choose the best possible route for each project. After all, a career isn't built on one book.

There are many ways you can get your book into the hands of a reader. You can go the route via an agent, to a big company, and wait to be rejected from them or multiple publishers. You can submit directly to a major publisher without an agent (I strongly recommend *The Writer's Market* book for an up to date listing of publishers, it has tons of good data like doing cover letters to inquire). You can do the small press route, where you submit directly to the editor or publisher like mine, Dark Moon Press, if your works fit their genre (visit www.darkmoonpress.com). You can also go the self-publishing route where you do everything yourself. There's also the "hybrid" route that takes bits and pieces from all of the above. The hybrid approach, which is what many authors have done, where you write books traditionally to get a name and once you feel you have recognition you want more control and more money per copy. You set forth to do POD while your established books generate steady royalty checks twice a year or, you can do what I did, and reverse it, earn a name, and get a larger company to add your new work to their catalog so you can just write while focusing more time on promotion and events while not having to format covers and the rest.

Either way you want to do it is not wrong, but you have to figure which one works the best for you. Regardless of your choice, it is critical to keep writing. Not only does writing more books make you a better if you heed your editor's advice, but people discover your writing when you have more titles for them to purchase.

The important thing is that you, the creator, are empowered to choose, per project, how you would like to progress.

*Extra Tips and a Timeline for your Release*
Your book publicity begins with your title and a great cover!

It used to be that a cover wasn't created for some time, but, with people needing to see and get the excitement built, the sooner you have a cover the better in order to build interest and excitement. You can get it to book stores, interviewers who use it on announcements when they want to interview you, and it goes a long way in many aspects of publicity. Generate a social media buzz by revealing your book cover to your audience, especially if you have a few cover options in mind. You could launch a social media poll and have your followers and fans vote on their favorite. This helps make the fans feel involved and excited so they want it more. I also cover, in Social Media Marketing, how to best go over this as well as ads.

If you don't have artistic or design abilities it's worth the money to hire a professional cover designer. You can take photos yourself, ask permission of other photographers (but you'll usually have to pay them several hundred dollars), or you can purchase rights to a photo through ShutterStock, or similar companies, and design your own cover. Being an artist, I occasionally paint cover art and take high res photos then add text effects with MS Publisher or have a friend make it even better with Adobe Photoshop, or better yet, have one professionally done so it really stands out.

IF you design your own cover, as a self-published author, I can pass on a lot of information. After having published two hundred books with my company, Dark Moon Press, I tend to speed up the process and use a lot of self-created templates.

Once you complete your FINAL revision (that means, you've gone through a thorough writing and rewriting process, printing the manuscript on paper and marking it up in pen at least once), then, and only then, does it make sense to start your timeline.

*Final proofreading*
Send the book to a proofreader. I recommend hiring a professional, even though it can be quite expensive. If you want readers and reviewers to look at your work with respect, then give your book what it deserves: a professional, polished proofreading.

Most editors will charge between $1,000 - $2,000. I ended up hiring an editor for less than $300, but had it rechecked by two others. Much later I spared their wrath by installing a program called Grammarly which catches tons of errors, along with MS Word, for proofreading, before giving it to my editors.

It really may be worth making solid writing friends and exchanging editorial support with one another.

*Register ISBN*
It used to be that you absolutely had to buy a bundle of 10 ISBN numbers so you can use the remaining ones for future books or various formats. You can purchase and register your book's ISBN through Bowker.

Now you can get your ISBN included via several print on demand companies, like CreateSpace and Lulu.

Research

Begin researching websites and places you plan to incorporate into your marketing plan. Create a document where you can keep and edit/grow this list.

A press kit is important

Most major book reviewers will require a press kit or single sell sheet for your book. What needs to go on a book sell sheet? It should include the following:

- Author bio

- Book description

- Picture of the book's cover

- Any book reviews (if you have any in advance)

- Publication date

- ISBN

- Page count

- Print format

- Retail price

- Marketing information (Information that may validate you as an author or the book itself. If you have them, use awards.)

- Contact information

*Production*

Hopefully, you can start this sooner if you've given yourself more time. By now, your book should have been proofed and completely edited. This is the time to create your Kindle (or ePUB) version of the book, along with formatting the book for print.

Order your initial case!

Once your book is proofread and corrected is the time to order your first stash of books (25-50 copies, depending on how ambitious you are, how aggressive you want to be, and how many you can afford). I send radio interviewers and bloggers digital copies because it saves me money and saves them time in not having to wait for it.

Start building your mailing distribution list

This can be time-consuming research, and there are companies such as Meltwater that allow you access to news contact lists for a fee. The cost can be steep though, so if you have the time, start building your own list. Start local, compiling a list of news outlets in your area, then expand from there. IMPORTANT: Be targeted. Include only email addresses that might actually be interested in the arts or authors. Include libraries, as well, in your distribution.

Connect and network locally

See the section on Your First Appearance!

Two months from publication date, send out releases and do a follow up email the next month to make sure they have recieved it or if they need any more information. This is the perfect time to start lining up interviews with radio and internet podcasters.

Hopefully by now some of those book reviews have begun to trickle in. Update your press release and start sending it out. Create a news media buzz.

Hopefully, you will have been implementing your social media marketing throughout these months, but as the official book reviews come back, this is a great time to link and share those reviews across social media. Keep your attention going, people don't always see things right away and may need reminded, and often. It used to take four times of seeing something to prompt people to buy, now marketing experts will tell you it can take eight times or more, so keep promoting.

*Book Launch*
Promote this most of all.

Once the book is officially launched, play around with some discounts and free downloads, promoting them across various sites.

The list of marketing options below is not an official endorsement by me. I have not tried some of these and I've listed them simply for your consideration. I located them, simply, with several Google searches.

Some Book Marketing Options:

Book Reviewers

Some of these are free, others are a bit on the expensive side. Create a budget for yourself and don't go overboard. Stick to the budget.

Booklist (Submit 4 months in advance)
Price: FREE
Turnaround: 15 weeks
Midwest Book Review (Submit 3-4 months in advance)
Price: $50
Turnaround: 14-16 weeks

BookLife / Publisher's Weekly (Submit 3-4 months in advance)
Price: FREE
Turnaround: 12-15 weeks

Library Journal (Submit 3-4 months in advance)
Price: FREE
Turnaround: 3-4 months

Indie Reader Reviews (Submit 2-3 months in advance)
Price: $225 / $300
Turnaround: 5-9 weeks / 4-6 weeks

Portland Book Review (Submit 1-3 months in advance)
Price: FREE / $100 / $175
Turnaround: Unknown / 6-10 weeks / 3-4 weeks

Book Reporter (Submit 2 months in advance)
Price: FREE
Turnaround: Unknown

Foreword Review (Submit 2 months in advance)
Price: FREE
Turnaround: 2 months

Clarion Review (Submit 2 months in advance)
Price: $499

Turnaround: 4-6 weeks

Reader Views (Submit 1 month in advance)
Price: $119 (Other packages available)
Turnaround: 3 weeks

Independent Publisher (Submit 2 months in advance)
Price: FREE
Turnaround: 4-6 weeks
Self-Publishing Book Review (Submit 1 month in advance)
Price: $125
Turnaround: 30 days

BookReview.com (Submit by 1 month in advance)
Price: $45 (New Author Listing) / $185 (Express Review)
Turnaround: 2-3 weeks

Fiverr Book Reviews (Submit after publication date)
NOTE: This is a highly controversial option. Tread carefully.
Price: $5-10 each
Turnaround: Varies

Rated Reads (Submit 1 month in advance)
Price: FREE
Turnaround: Unknown

Sign up with Net Galley (Submit after publication)
NOTE: This websites connects authors with a community of authors, so
there is a possibility for a large number of reviews
Price: $399
Turnaround: Unknown

Nothing Binding (Submit anytime)
Price: FREE
Turnaround: Unknown

Readers Favorites (Submit anytime)
Price: FREE
Turnaround: Unknown

Book Promotion & Marketing Options

Author Marketing Club
A list of various FREE book promotion options
Library Bub
Email distribution list, marketing your book to 10,000 libraries
Price: $299 (but they often run specials at $149)

Many Books
Get featured on a newsletter sent to 110,000 subscribers
Price: $25 / $35

*Handling rejection*

Charlaine Harris's best-selling vampire mysteries, The Sookie Stackhouse Novels became the basis for the HBO series, *True Blood*, which ran on HBO for six seasons. However it wasn't always roses for her, in the beginning Charlaine's manuscript agent, Joshua Bilmes, said he had a hard time selling the first Sookie book and that it was rejected by a dozen publishers. They were not receptive. A lot of them said, 'We think it's well written, but we're not sure where to shelve it." The original novels have sold more than 32 million copies globally. Persistence pays off. I have had two books rejected from two different companies, until 2009 when Schiffer Publishing picked up *Cemetery Gates Death and Mourning through the Ages*. I went from being self-published to starting a small publishing company to now putting out 130 titles by more than thirty authors before my name meant anything to my editor at Schiffer. If I ever needed validation I finally had it. You see, when you have the power to put anything out, in our day and age of print on demand, sometimes it is nice to know a 'real' publisher likes your work just as much. I will say though, that had they not, I would always have the satisfaction of knowing I already had built a fan base with my dozen books before that. Rejection can be crushing, but if you love to write, get over it and do what you love. The old saying is true, do what you love and the money will follow.

## Self-esteem and confidence

In order to make any use of the advice in this, you have to believe in yourself, even if it means building a larger than life ego. Oprah Winfrey said she saw herself as an instrument of will, knowing she was destined for greatness. Even the most egotistical and powerful people in the world know it isn't entirely true but they act as if they are. Gene Simmons says, "If you're the greatest, it's okay to say you're the greatest. My suggestion to everybody is to be their own greatest fan. Weaker personas and personalities define that as egotistical or arrogant, but what it means is their self-esteem isn't that strong." Having good self-esteem leads to confidence and,in turn, creates a positive self-image. You either are one of us who will go after it or you don't have it in you, stop the bus and get off. All people are not equal, not everyone has Schwarzenegger's Olympian potential. The saying "we are all equal" is a fairy tale to keep the lesser people content while they stay on the bottom. If you don't like it, find a path to make yourself happy and use what you do have – know your limitations and focus on your natural strengths.

## Confronting what holds you back

By working from the inside out and focusing on changing your own way of thinking - which you must do before changing the circumstances around you - you develop a more positive self-concept. This is done while seeing yourself honestly, by deliberately removing the internal barriers that can keep you from doing your best.

Fellow author, Michelle Belanger, told me once, "We are our own biggest roadblocks to our success and happiness." I discovered she was right, by looking at my fears which held me back and others who repeatedly failed to believe in themselves to force themselves out of the viscous cycle of fear and failure. Another friend, Aaron W. "Storm" Anderson, explained his thoughts in dealing with getting past obstacles versus how most people act when he encounters them in his tattoo shop, "Nearly every day I'm at the shop, someone begins a sentence with, 'I wish...' The reality is that over 90% of those people will never have more than a wish or a prayer. My wife and I don't live in a big house (yet) or drive really fancy cars, but we have definitely accomplished some pretty cool things. Not a single accomplishment began with, 'I wish.' ALL of them started with a Goal followed by a realistic plan that we immediately put into action. Our Magic is real, but it isn't hocus-pocus. It's supported directly by creativity, strategy, determination, and because goals always take time, patience."

Attitude has much to do with, not only how we think of ourselves, but with how we present ourselves on the outside. This trait is character. Dwelling on the past, whether it be life's hardships, mishaps, or personal mistakes, does nothing good for you but certainly does put wear and tear on you, mentally and physically. If we spend too much time on what we didn't do right, how will we move forward? True, we cannot excel without first understanding what caused the problems, but there are limits. A positive attitude shouldn't be confused with total arrogance, for that has the flaw of becoming blind to important warning signs.

# Publicity: Marketing Yourself

When we get caught up in the excitement of being in print for the first time, you have to remember that publishing is a business, authors need to see themselves as businessmen and women, because the publishing industry of our day and age requires those who are serious to take on the extra responsibility of treating their writing and their publishing as their business, because it is. It is about making money, which takes marketing (know your audience), sales and PR (direct sales to people) and advertising (flyers, radio interviews) for example. As people in our busy world, we are inundated with advertising and most people just tune it out.

Even though the internet makes the world seem smaller, we are flooded with not only more information to deal with but with more competition. With changes for the better in self-publishing, more people are doing it. I have a lot of thoughts on that, but will get into that in the section on self-publishing and traditional publishing.

Promotion Devoid of Connection is Pointless.

One big complaint from authors is they feel their book isn't doing well because of a lack of promotion. Have realistic expectations from the publisher. Yes, they do promote, but there are activities they must do on their end to make those promotions effective. Return on investment in business is simple, regarding promotion and advertising.

Effort devoid of action from the author equals failure, simple logic.

We can create the world's most elaborate website but without people knowing it exists in the first place, it is pointless. You must create a fan base. We gravitate to companies/personal brands, remember you are one, you are a real person behind the tweets and posts. This is what is called platform building, in our digital age it is built on social media and marketing yourself. If you don't care the audience won't either. They will look you up and see you aren't online promoting, doing events in person or getting interviews. Why would they buy your book if you have no passion to tell them about it? You yourself will put more enthusiasm into talking about it than anyone else possibly could.

You must help yourself. That's right, I know from selling books at conventions, at book signings at stores versus my royalties from a much bigger company I write for may be many times bigger than Dark Moon Press, but my check is much smaller than what I can get on my own, Why? Because I care to get it out there and make people care about it more than anyone – and you should too, or why did you create it?

Publishers should create customized promotions; I always listen to my writers' suggestions because authors sometimes have great ideas in relation to promotion on their books that I might not have thought of. Authors not only know their topic, but also are in various clubs, social media groups so they know where their fans are better than anyone.

Look at other known authors, see what they do and copy them! Watch motivational speaking videos on YouTube. That's right, I know it can be unnerving to think about, I can relate. You are an introverted author who types away from the public, and you think that now you are done and can remain hidden away from people and make a good living. WRONG. Your book is done and now is the time to switch hats and be your own biggest salesman. Worries about public speaking and how to do a signing event? Not to worry, we cover that in the lessons ahead.

Pay attention to what methods work on any social media site. LinkedIn, Twitter, Facebook, it is irrelevant doesn't matter, you need a solid plan that will work with any as they come and go – remember MySpace? The theory works on Tumbler and Twitter, Facebook and the next big one that comes along too – when you build a fan base/platform will remain intact and continue to grow with you.

Realize things change! Adapt and overcome, pay attention to what other authors are doing. Follow in the footsteps of those you admire. Large companies are realizing Facebook can be an asset and that people don't want endless spam and promotion. We want a company that includes us and represents our values. We are willing to pay more to those kinds of companies. We want to like who we buy from.

*Authors Have to Market Themselves!*
There is a distinction between a business and a real person, but the lines blur when you are a writer. All of us on some level we all are required to market ourselves. When we apply for a job, we know that we have to wear the right clothing, the right smile and have the right answers in an interview if we want to land the job. In very much the same way, you need to put your best foot forward and do the same when we put ourselves out there when marketing ourselves to the public, so people will relate to us, like us and listen to us so they will buy our work.

When it comes to creating a "marketable author brand" I am not trying to change you as a person, just polish your style to help in how you get attention.

We don't like people who promote themselves in person, the endless braggart. The same goes for when you have a presence on-line. People have to care about what you do both in life and as an author, so share a bit of you so they will feel a connection to you. If they follow you on any social media it is not to be 'sold to'. If we only appear just when we have a book for sale, you become huckster and nobody cares what you have to say, it is just another ad to turn off.

Don't get me wrong, you do need to promote and frequently, just mix it up with other posts that aren't directly related to your work. It will make it so that when you are in public, people will come to see you because they like you! Fans buy your books because they value what they can learn from you or are entertained by you in a work of fiction, but to a large degree if they like you, your short stories about life you post online and pictures of your cat doing something cute. Fans are excited in getting the chance to see you, they will come to your classes at events and get a signature on a book of yours. What you just sold them was your presence and a great memory…what they have is a handful of paper and ink that later has meaning once they read it. Why? Because they want that connection to deepen. This is why TV stars and movie actors have swarms of fans at conventions. They want to see you, hear you and know you looked into their eyes when you smiled and shook their hands! That is building a relationship. Online is no different.

## Building an Author Platform

Author platform is one of the most difficult concepts to explain, partly because everyone defines it a little differently. But by far the easiest explanation is: an ability to sell books because of who you are or who you can reach. This section is pretty in depth because it is how you connect with your fans, outside of meeting you and reading your work.

A platform is the most valuable thing an author can have.

And the time to start building that platform is now.

Of course, your next question is: How do I build a platform?

It has a lot of parts but to make it simple, it comes down to three main things:

Permission. You need to have a way to communicate with your fans that reliably gets their attention and drives them into action. Adding them, getting them to follow you on social media is critical.

Content. You need to put your work out into the world widely and freely, for people to easily find and interact with.

You need a way to move people from not knowing you exist to knowing you are everywhere. By maintaining a presence you make it easy for them to give you permission to stay in contact long-term. Fans will love your content of that post and want to see more from you.

These three steps can happen in so many different ways.

For example, they hear you speak at a conference, they loved your talk and want to learn more or they read your guest post on a blog they read regularly.

*Strategies vs. Tactics*
Tactics will change over time, but Strategy always stays the same.

Here's a strategy: Do Outreach, Share Content, and Get Permission.

Here's a tactic: Connect with a blogger, write a guest post, and then invite readers of the post to join your email list. Get a spot speaking at a conference, share great information there, then invite people to join your email list.

When you reach out to others with great content, your following grows. It can be as easy as fans sharing your posts, to new people hearing you are a convention and on radio podcasts. I know I have gained thousands of fans this way.

Be aware that tactics come and go. Tactics change. Tactics are personal choices.

But Strategy is universal, and always stays the same.

So where do tactics come in, and what tactics should you use?

This is where it gets tricky. Because there are just so many options for what you could be spending your time on.

Blogging, podcasting, Twitter, Facebook, Pinterest, LinkedIn, Forums, and Goodreads, to name a few.

And confusingly, there's too much advice on how to use any one of those options.

How often should you blog? What length should the posts be? Should they have photos or graphics, how often do you post inspiring memes or cute animal pictures? Should your posts contain links leading to other websites?

You will figure it out best by trying all of it and watching the reactions (emoticons), the amount of likes, and comments versus the ones you try that get the least. This takes time to see patterns.

An author platform is the answer of 'Who you are."

Why YOU (why your book)?

Why not someone else?

What do you offer ME?

What makes you so special?

WHO ARE YOU and why does the consumer care?

Everything in life is a business. Relating to people, selling your work, selling your own branding of who 'you' are is sales and marketing. People have to care about you, what you know, what you are trying to share. Yet, the smart writer understands that making a living doing what we love involves good business sense.

I have studied both in business college, marketing, advertising, communication and good business people know anything in sales forces the maker of the product to become a sustainable brand that connects to the buyer, and in this case it is our readers. I make good use of this with Dark Moon Press in a carefully laid plan for branding and blogging that has proven to work time and time again and has helped sell over a hundred titles my company has.

Writers need a meaningful and effective social media platform for that will last for years. I started out as a one book guy now I am drafting ideas for number my thirtieth title. But it took time to build a following of my name. People see the penname and ask for me for conventions, gravitate to my lectures. Why? Because they know of me. You need to develop that and this will give you the steps. Remember, readers gravitate to who/what we know and like.

Do not discount your personal persona, or the importance of the first question, of are you so special? What do you offer that will make someone buy you book in the sea of other books on the market? The N.Y. Time book reviewers receive a thousand books every single week to look at. Think about that.

As authors, understand the buyer who visits Amazon or B&N.com wants to know, "Why should I get your book, when there are a million others to pick from?"

How and where should you try to get noticed? Everywhere, but narrow it down. Think about where you see people and concepts, online, in stores, bulletin boards. Think outside of just doing local bookstore signings. Flyers in your hometown are good but do it where the clientele is laid back, like a coffee house bulletin board not a shopping mall or grocery when people just want to buy and go. Think libraries, they buy books so inquire at your local library, ask readers services about putting a copy on their shelf, it is free advertising for you to thousands of people looking for a book like yours who might check it out and leave it out where others see it. They will pick it up, become interested and maybe go get one for themselves or for a friend as a gift. I occasionally donate a free copies to local library so more people will get to see my work for the first time.

People in everyday life – if you are personal and involve yourself with them let them know you wrote a book they might want a copy but they will never know unless you tell them, so always keep copies in your car. You never know who you might run into!

Where can you find a niche audience just waiting for you to see them? To connect with them?

Exploit the personal and professional connections you have, make full use of your email address book, make use of the business cards you pick up at events and especially any radio interviews you may have done in the past if you put out another book. When you release future titles, stay in touch with all the people you know. Just because someone didn't buy one of your books doesn't mean they won't buy your next one.

Any media outlets (including blogs and social networks) that you can utilize to sell or at least advertise to push your books.

## Social Media Marketing

Social media is the collective of online communications channels dedicated to community-based input, interaction, content-sharing and collaboration.

Websites and applications dedicated to forums, microblogging, social networking, social bookmarking, social curation, and wikis are among the different types of social media.

Success in social media is the result of building a long term connection with your fans who become repeat customers. In today's world where everyone is glued to their phone, it is increasingly difficult to get people to sit down and read a book, or at times, even a ebook, so it is vital you reach as many people as possible. At least 75% of people us social media, and in order to maximize it to your full advantage as an author, outside of creating an account of every kind available to spread your brand it is important to know where your brand thrives.

You get more followers here on a steady basis; it is what keeps people involved in your life. Go where people are, in the real world and online. And that means social media. FaceBook, Twitter, Instagram, blogging, and yes, even – or especially, YouTube.

### Facebook

Facebook, my best friend. No I am only half joking. I make 50% of my income due to marketing to a growing my fan base on social media. There are a lot of things you can do to make the most of your profile on Facebook.

Video tape yourself at conventions giving a speech. I actually have an assistant who records me at events (see Conventions) so that I not only advertise where I have been a speaker at, like DragonCon, and it also establishes you on your websites when new people encounter you and want to see what it is you do. They want to see you in action, to know you are worth having at their event.

This is where it comes into play on a 24-7 type of notoriety that keeps spreading who you are even as you sleep.

Make a FaceBook page, not a personal profile. Authors especially need the added perks built into a professional page, like businesses have. You get options of a custom web address, especially to match your author official site, and it lets you run ads. From this your followers get to see much more of what you post make sure you use a great cover and profile picture, something that makes you stand out. You can do a call to action.

Pages are an important destination for people on Facebook, and we're building new ways for people to interact with businesses through them. Today, we're announcing a new call-to-action feature that will help Pages drive business objectives.

Designed to bring a business's most important objective to the forefront of its Facebook presence, call-to-action buttons link to any destination on or off Facebook that aligns with a business's goals.

Page admins can select from a group of call-to-action buttons — like Shop Now or Sign Up — to add to the top of their Page. The seven calls to action available are:


Book Now

Contact Us

Use App

Play Game

Shop Now

Sign Up

Watch Video

This helps communicate who you are, it encourages fans to add themselves to your page, to follow you, and add themselves to your email list. You can use a service like mailchimp. As their website reads:

"More than 14 million people and businesses around the world use MailChimp. Our features and integrations allow you to send marketing emails, automated messages, and targeted campaigns. And our detailed reports help you keep improving over time.

"MailChimp has been around since 2001. The company started as a side project funded by various web-development jobs. Now we're the world's leading email marketing platform, and we send more than a billion emails a day. We democratize technology for small businesses, creating innovative products that empower our customers to grow.

"When you connect your store with one of MailChimp's hundreds of e-commerce integrations, you can create targeted campaigns, automate helpful product follow-ups, and send back-in-stock messaging. Learn what your customers are purchasing, then send them better email."

You can also customize your tabs and rearrange the order of them, by clicking 'change' to upload a new image. By adding FaceBook plugins, share buttons on your website (as well as Twitter and other quick links to your social media) you official .com can get a lot more exposure.

Once you have built your various pages and profiles, no matter which ones you use, update them with content as often as you can. People have a short term memory and get bombarded constantly with new information, cuddly cat videos and silly memes, not to mention a slew of ads and articles.

Cross post to as many of them as you can. In order to maximize your time, make use of a many that can be done at a time. I know my Instagram account is tied into my official author FaceBook account and Twitter so all I need to do is upload a book cover or where I am and make a post with hastags, and scroll down slightly and check FaceBook and Twitter, and it posts to all three. I then copy it to my personal profile on FaceBook and out of 5,000 friends I know over 1,000 actively follow me there with a 200-400 who interact with me on a regular basis. Also, I share my YouTube videos to my FaceBook and Twitter accounts to get more views. My cell phone and GoPro both offer immediate broadcasting, and of course you also can make use of Periscope on Twitter and FaceBook Live. I highly recommend you use the best lighting and sound as you can possibly get out of it, as fans get annoyed when they can't see or hear you at a cool event or doing a talk they are missing out on while you are at a convention. Be consistent in posting, as not everyone is all on at all times of the day, or even every day at all. Those who do check their feed do so for only about a half hour to an hour at a time, and just about 11% of your fans actually see what you post anyway without you paying for ads to increase the likelihood of it reaching more. I count myself lucky I reach about 30% of my fans per post. Most social media, and FaceBook especially use algorithms in order to judge if your fans are interested in what you post, out of a thousand posts they can view in an hour. Make use of services like Buffer (www.buffer.com) and paying $10 a month helps you reach a dozen platforms from a single dashboard, so saving time is worth the money. Scheduling posts ahead saves you time, especially helpful in making the most of your time while you are on the road, or speaking at a panel at a convention while doing a panel. First, you are at a convention, like DragonCon, which is prestigious enough, and on a panel so even to new attendees unfamiliar with you (see conventions in this course) you look like an expert. Your panel could be streamed live, shared while you mention a new book you did, and a multiple post can be seen of it and spread around. A new book on the topic of the convention could be seen by a few thousand in one evening if done like this. I sold a book in 2016 at DragonCon, all 50 copies I had on me sold, three stores contacted me for copies to sell and I landed a book signing before I left town. These super posts can catch older fans up on what you have been up to later if you 'pin' a video like this to the top of your professional FaceBook page (I did this) and new fans get to see you. It also causes browsers to see how well you conduct yourself on a professional level, which in turn can get you more convention to make new fans, get you TV spots, more radio interviews and networking!

*Paying for ads on FaceBook*

It turns out when you target Facebook ads to fans, you get 700% more click throughs, according the data king Webtrends. Additional data from TGB Digital shows that ads targeted at fans increases actual conversions (not just click) by as much as 400%.

Yes, you need to build an audience first, and yes, increasing your fan engagement helps support any future conversion efforts. But ultimately, when you want to convert with Facebook ads, targeting fans is the way to go. The data does not lie. You have a split second to get my attention with a Facebook ad. If it isn't clear that this ad is relevant to me in any way, I'll immediately turn my attention elsewhere.

Therefore, communicating relevance in the ad is extremely important I tend to do one or two ads off of my professional FaceBook account per month that a new title has come out or art print I do. I don't go over $200 on any one ad, and usually limit myself to $100 to reach 6,000 or so. I only once spent $300 on an ad, but it was accompanied by a heavily calculated combination of tricks that all worked. I had a video of me speaking at a convention, debuting a book I know was already selling very well and I had links to order it in the description, along with a sale of but two books in the set and get the full $20 DVD free. People love videos, it makes them click it (I am still getting views, 14,000 watched in under a year and it is still being shared and complimented), people love to see you in action, and that many views and shares/likes/comments builds your trust to new fans, gains you chances to be seen by yet more people. "buy and get FREE" helps also, so it was a very calculated and formulated move. However, if you are just starting out and do not have a wide enough fan base, I don't recommend paying for it. Build your fan base first to make it worth it. Also, see how much organic reach you get in the first five hours before you boost a post, let it climb before you pay to expand its reach. When we surveyed social marketers on the future of social media marketing as an industry we found that Facebook and Facebook ads are a huge focus for most businesses. And still, many businesses are not following some of these simple social advertising best practices. Always split-test your ads, let your ads run for a longer time period than a couple days, and don't miss out of some of Facebook's best targeting options.

The pricing of Facebook ads is based on an auction system where ads compete for impressions based on bid and performance. When you run your ad, you'll only be charged for the number of clicks or the number of impressions your ad received.

You can estimate the cost before you create your ad by looking at what we recommend you bid for each click (CPC) or thousand impressions (CPM).

To estimate the cost of your ad for clicks or impressions before you create it:

Go to ad creation.

Go through the steps to create an ad and select Show Advanced Options for what you would like to do with your ad.

In the Campaign Pricing section under Bidding, select Optimize for clicks or Optimize for impressions.

The bid estimator will appear and show you the range of bids that are currently winning the auction among ads similar to yours.

Based on this estimate, you can determine how much you wish to spend per click or per thousand impressions. You can multiply that number by the number of clicks or thousand impressions you wish to receive each day to determine your approximate daily budget. The amount that you're charged each day will never exceed the daily budget that you set.

If you run your ad, our system will only charge you the minimum amount required to win that placement, which may be less than your maximum bid. Because we lower the cost on your behalf, we recommend that you enter your true maximum bid when creating an ad. This will increase the likelihood that don't miss out on the clicks or impressions that you otherwise could have received as the required bid fluctuates.

Adding a Call-to-Action to your Facebook Ads might not increase your click-through rate or make your ad more engaging, but it's likely to improve your overall conversion rate and decrease your cost per conversion.

Why? Because a good call-to-action decreases friction. If a user clicks your ad and arrives on your landing page, it won't need to waste time figuring what to do next. He'll already know and quickly proceed to perform the desired action.

He'll know because you've prompted him in your Ad with a Call-to-Action like "Download our eBook...," "Subscribe to our newsletter for a chance to win...," "Take the survey and receive $10 off...," etc.

*Address your users' rational and emotional sides.*

We think we're intelligent animals who always act rationally, but that's only partially true. Our emotional side has a lot to say when it comes to buying.

A simple list of product features might convince the rational self in some users but has no effect at all on their emotional self. Our emotional self-doesn't care about features, that part of us wants benefits. In your Facebook Ad designs, use the psychology of color to your advantage.

If you're not harnessing the psychological powers that different colors can have, then you're missing out on a vital creative force that every top Facebook ads pro is using.

Nearly 90% of all the snap judgments that we make about products can be traced back to color, according to a study in Management Decision. Here are some of the major science-backed trends in how people perceive colors that you should keep in mind:

Older people like blue, purple, and green, while younger people are more into yellow, red, and orange. As we age, our preferences tend towards the darker and cooler colors of shorter wavelength over the excitatory, long wavelength colors.

When planning out your ad creative and deciding on a color to use, think about the market you're selling to, what they like, what they expect, and then you'll be thinking along the right lines.

Check out what your competitors are doing. Look at what is working. Subtle changes in color can influence how we see advertising, so take your time and make your decisions count.

Be sure to keep an eye on your analytics after the ads, so you can tell if certain type of ads did better than others (doing a picture of your book with a url on it, the price etc helps), but don't ever pay for an ad of just text.

You can also use Google Analytics Network Referrals for "Social Mention" tracking of your name ad company or whatever is trending connected to you.

Never pay for fans or 'Get followers fast" scams, as they will be filled with bots, and people who do not share your interests. It is far better to have 100 to 1,000 true fans that spread your name than pay for false leads.

Some advice on what to post.

Humanize who you are to your fans. Don't just shout BUY MY BOOK constantly, even though you are excited about a release, or want as many sales as possible as quickly as possible. It is wise to share every aspect of your life, since human beings are voueyers and want to get to know you as a person not just as a writer. Share your food, your cats (I do this often, my fans know my cats names and personalities) post-holiday decorations (but not your home address in the photos, there are stalkers!!). Fans want to know you, that connecting brings them to care about you, as much as realities shows became a huge hit, they get that same level of wanting to know the authors they cherish. This isn't to say you shouldn't push your books, by all means do so but stick as much as you can to a 80/20 rule of only 20% posts about your book itself. We will cover that as well, on how best to make use of that when you do. Your content should resonate what you understand their wants, needs and desires out of you. Images get 180% more views, and videos even more than that in comparison to just words. When you do just post words, make them funny, deeply philosophical, entertaining or useful to your reader. They have to feel like they need to click on what you post and keep up with you. Show behind the scenes, of your travels, at conventions, as you create. I have shared screen shots of books being made, series of images of my art as it is being painted. THIs builds excitement and hype, shares and more sales of your work. Fans like to see things like this, it is why we watch the extras on a movie DVD.

Special note:

FaceBook puts priority on video uploaded by their site versus YouTube, so switch between both if you have each type of account to maximize both social media platforms. FaceBooks videos play automatically and they mute them in the news feed.

Organize the videos you put up into play lists via your video tab on your page to encourage increased watch times, and choose one to Feature. This one will appear in the prime spot below the About section. If you do a great presentation and do a clip of it, have this be your calling card so others want to bring you to their event, college or book you as a speaker. Add descriptive tags to make each one stand out. In 2016 Facebook started its Live Feed feature worldwide to record up to 30 min of video. You can write up a brief description and choose what audience to share it with. You can see how many live viewers you have, read comments in real time and save the video for later.

Chat in communities, post in groups. Get known as an expert on a topic, build up their trust in you and get them to know and like what you say as you slip in your a writer.in that way you add the type of niche genre of fan you want to attract to you, they like your posts and share things you post. These are the people who become your die-hard fans.

Emoticons equal 33% more likes, comments and shares. When you make your posts meaningful it causes emotional triggers. Get fans involved. Get people's opinions, I have done that and discovered what next book to write just by inquiring or posting a mock up cover to build advance hype! It is far better to spend half a year writing what you know dozens to hundreds of fans already want than releases something in hopes they might like it.

Start discussions. Make use of breaking news flashes in the media and find a way to tie into you or something you have done (be a bit subtle) holidays. For example, I publish books and do art on Krampus. Especially when the movie just came out, I tied in several books, original paintings, prints and post cards. Let's just say Christmas was merrier than it had been in years after I did that!

Using images that are not yours for attention.

This is tricky. You can do this and add text, make your own memes for attention. I recommend vectorfree.com, yaymicro.com, vectorstock.com compflight.com, freeimages.com. Always pay attention to the sites terms of uses.

Of course, your own brand, author picture, company logo is great to build brand recognition, and the consistency in colors, styles, themes, logos and url is important. I use the one form my official author website and made my Twitter look exactly like it for that reason and at least twice a year switch to it on my FaceBook.

Keep track of the number of engagements to your pages, you usually get a weekly email notifying you of the traffic and level of engagement with your fans you get. It will show ratings up or down from prior weeks, amount of post reach which types of updates got the most views, age, gender so you know how to tweak posts to pull in your desired fan base.

Some other important points to keep in mind:

Do you know what the most influential emotion in a purchase decision is? Fear.

People resist buying your product because they're scared of losing money and afraid of making the wrong choice. This is why free products are so effective and 'limited time offer' because they fear missing out. Companies like to use sayings like, "New" and "Limited Time Offer."

Of course, I'm not suggesting that you should give your product away for free (although sometimes you should). I'm just suggesting that you need to address customers' fears by adding Social Proofs to your Facebook Ad Designs.

A great social proof that reduces fear are testimonials from famous people. Having an endorsement or testimonials, your product immediately gives you credibility and removes a level of fear. If you don't have testimonials, you can still leverage your large user base. People love special offers, so using a discount code, especially with a time limit creates a sense of urgency so if they are on the fence and have seen your ad or mention of something appear online more of them take advantage of discounts. I know for a fact those of you who jumped on the $100 off prep ay in full made a big difference in the number of people who signed up for both of my classes.

There's nothing we hate more than losing out on a great deal because we were just a little bit late. It's the principle of loss aversion: we feel bad when we miss out on getting something, but we feel even worse about losing. And when we see an urgent opportunity arise, we do not want to let it slip through our fingers.

One of the biggest problems with advertising today is that urgency can be difficult to trigger in people. Since we can get items in less than 5 hours off Amazon and virtually every other e-commerce platform offers some 1-2 day shipping options, people feel as though they can probably get whatever they want whenever they want.

Inducing scarcity and urgency could mean grabbing hold of your audience's attention with an eye-catching deal that they just can't pass up. You want to create a deep sense of FOMO—fear of missing out.

This also works very well when you want to sell signed discounted copies of your book (or offer signed and free shipping) around the holidays.

Upcoming events should be emphasized, advertised a few times in advance, and if you can, post them as an event on Facebook so people get reminders. Book launches, store signings and major television debuts of you are critical to do this with. All of these should be done with an image or banner ad on the page to grab attention just as effective as billboards on the side of the road.

Contests and giveaways help a lot. People love the word FREE remember, and the excitement they might be a winner pushes them to pay attention to what you are doing.

Show images of fans with your book, have them post them on their social media and tag you in it, this gets more attention and is a he endorsement for you on non-mutual friends will be attracted to you and it gets more sales for you. I know I have gained new fans of my books, fundraisers and artwork sold over the years because of fans sharing posts of art on their walls or books on their night stands.

Net working with what is called influencers (higher known celebrities) can help you if they get to know you and like what you do. If you engage in conversations with them on their feed and they endorse your work, share your page. This takes time to build so do not rush into it. But if it is successful, it brings your mutual fan base together and gains both of you more exposure. Networking and collaborations help a lot, even in writing a book with co-authors. It also saves you time in getting the book done.

In 2013 Facebook allowed the use of hashtags joining the likes of Twitter, Pinterst, and Instagram. This group's similar content together for people to locate their interests quicker. This peeks at 8-11, especially Fri- Sunday which will get your events and releases more attention.

Directly ask your fans to share, like and repost your posts. I have gained a lot of attention for my books and events I am at simply by asking my fans to share a post. Just because you get hundreds of likes doesn't mean a thousand people will see what you post, but if you post in groups (I have done it in as many as a hundred groups) and asked a fans on all my social media simultaneously to repost and gained thousands of likes on a simple picture of a book cover. Don't assume they will do it on their own, you have to ask for the help and usually they will.

Add what's' known as milestones of your career and better yet, like asking them to add images with your book, ask fans to share milestones of how your work has helped them. People love to talk about themselves, so if your book truly was written to solve their problems (remember marketing and big sales, help others helps your bottom line) you fans will want to tell their story.

In the nature of helping others, cross promote other writers, work together, especially if you will all be at the same book store of convention! This lets fans know (you can tag each other on your walls in posts or tag them in a banner/photo from the convention flyer) I do this at the really big events especially if I know a lot of my friends see it. New fans of theirs and vice versa will see the ad and want to come out. This will gain both parties more sales.

*Twitter*
Authentic relationships will help us professionally. When we use social media properly, our names become tied to our line of work, to our product. This is how to make the most of it.

First things first. Set up a Twitter account. Even if you aren't ready to actually tweet anything, set up an account before you get too famous and someone uses your Twitter name for their account. (Optimism is a good thing!)

While Twitter can't sell books all by itself, it is one of the tools you can use to for promotion of your book. Some writers have used Twitter to tease their audience by clipping and posting sections of their book 140 characters at a time. I did the same thing with *Unlocking the Secrets of Control, Wealth and Power*, and in its first month I outsold that title ten to one to every book I put out that year all year. Don't forget to link to the page where readers can get your book, if you sell signed copies via Face Book, guide them to your PayPal account and every copy gets free shipping and autographed, I do this and also run special where if fans buy several books that way I throw in another free! This tactic works if you have a large quantity of your work on hand and a lot of different titles.

Vine is Twitter's new service that lets you capture and share short looping videos. Vine videos are only six seconds but they can get interest.

*YouTube*
Add your YouTube Video to Your Blog and Website

It is not complicated to create and account on YouTube and upload video files to your account. Usually the platform you do a blog or website on will give you clear step-by-step directions on how to add a YouTube video. As for your author website Wix.com is great for those of us without the skills to do html coding. You can gain new exposure simply by having a YouTube account but be sure and invite people to follow you on all of your social media. YouTube has followers, the fans will share your videos and you should always include you official site at the end with your publishers url. It is important to do it at the end, because if they liked you they will go to it to buy, and if you have it in the beginning they won't remember it at all by the time the video is over. So do yourself a favor and after you do a official website do this too!

## 6 Steps to Creating a Branded YouTube Channel

Learn how you can launch a YouTube channel for your business -- even if you aren't a video expert.

Entrepreneur Network partner Mark Fidelman of Fanatics Media explains how to create a branded YouTube channel.

"Today, everything revolves around video. It's the best form for communicating with an audience, Fidelman explains.

"When you're first launching your YouTube channel, it's best to outsource elements such as lighting, editing and sound to experts. Once your business grows, you'll be able to take everything in-house, Fidelman says. If you don't have an on-camera talent, that's something that can be outsourced, too -- look for influencers in your industry who might be a good fit.

Creating the right content, incorporating relevant calls-to-action and utilizing analytics tools are other steps that will help jumpstart your new channel."

## Blogging

Blogging is an effective way to build your web presence, connect with customers and help new customers discover you. But be careful with official author sites and blogs – they can make you look like a rock star author or a failure! Avoid these things like I described about Twitter.

Keep your links to purchase easy to get to. Remember to think like a customer, they leave in three seconds if they can't find what gets them captivated or to make a purchase!

Take a look at websites and blogs by others who do what you do, pay attention to the colors and design features used. Be careful with your personal design, make sure it fits with how you want to be seen. I use the same picture and background design on my social media accounts as I have on my website, if one changes I do it to them all. Make it so people instantly 'know' who you are, remember you are a brand!

Just like with Twitter (and Facebook) your blog is not about you, it is about your fans, and your customers. Don't post only self-promotional your events, and releases, cover other things (related to your industry) things that will be interesting and useful to your fans.

So many authors, including those in my publishing company fail to promote. The best book ever is worthless and will not sell if it isn't promoted. Put the URL on printed materials, such as postcards, your banner at your table you set up at events and on the back covers of your books - encourage people to find you everywhere.

There are, of course, many other things you can do to promote a specific blog post or your blog overall. You can't do everything, but doing at least a few of these things on a regular basis will generate much more traffic to your blog and help you to reach more readers.

## Author Website

If you don't have a website, GET ONE.

Working in the self-publishing industry for many years, and the majority of authors I speak with always ask me the same question...

"Do I need a website as an independent author?"

And the answer I always tell them is... yes! Without a doubt.

Having a website establishes credibility for you as an author, helps to build your author brand, makes it easier to connect with your readers, and most importantly... helps you sell more books!

Make sure your author about me page is interesting and relevant.

If you truly want to be respected and sell, you have to have one for credibility. Register a domain. (GoDaddy is a good place to start.) I always recommend selecting "www.yourname.com," or if that is taken, then "www.yournameauthor.com." Just like with your Twitter handle, you want to make it easy for your fans to find you. I don't recommend going with www.nameofyourbook.com because when you write your follow up books it will be difficult for people to locate you. When someone hears about you they will do an online search, and you want your name or penname to be how they find you. I use www.corvisnocturnum.com.

Use testimonials! Post them on you official website people NEED to think you are in demand, are an expert, and have value for THEM. Take post cards; have business cards and other promotional materials advertising your books to every event, convention or college. Put them on bulletins boards in your home town and when you travel. I even stick them in mirrors of restrooms at gas stations and especially at conventions since you have a captive audience already, one of the tricks in guerilla marketing.

Think big and small combined tactically. Not only mass media national of internationally, but in daily life, or small shops, libraries. Every single sale has a ripple effect and touches others like a domino effect. Never overlook an opportunity, word of mouth matters just as much if not more.

It might be antiquated with the millions of people on social media, but I still hold to the idea you need a website to truly look professional to the public. If you don't have a website, GET ONE. If you truly want to be respected and sell, you have to have one for credibility. Register a domain. (GoDaddy is a good place to start.) I always recommend selecting www.yourname.com, or if that is taken, then www.yournameauthor.com or www.yournamebooks.com. Just like with your Twitter, you want to make it easy for your fans to find you. Never use the name of your first book as your websites name, because what happens when you write your second book? That may sound like crazy talk now, but it is quite possible that one day you will write a second book! (See my above note about optimism.)

Get links for radio, TV, which interview you did and make sure it is on your blogs, Twitter, Face Book and personal site. Have links on your website that lick directly to your social media locations. Take pictures of you at events. It is all for establishing credibility and awareness that you have indeed been a speaker at a convention and in demand. If you do not fewer people will care to get a hold of you for their event or show. Take a stack of cards or post cards to every event you do. Advertising it on the publishing site will cause an increase in traffic and all of the authors through the publishing company you do could use promotion – or if you self-publish you must do this.

Always add your press releases to your own author website. Add a media page to your site, with publicity photos, any major magazine stories where you have been featured in, copy your YouTube videos of you. People in the media that visit sites when they want to do an article, and when they feel you are an expert on what they want to push as news it helps immensely.

*Mailing lists and Mass emails*
Email marketing has been around for years and is till effective as a tool.

Never purchase a mailing list, they are a waste of money and you can even get your accounts shut down as a spammer. Add your book beneath in the "signature" of your personal e-mail account, same with your official author website. The signature is typically found in the "settings" section of any e-mail account.

## Amazon to boost Sales
Although I tend to ask my writers to get people to put the Dark Moon Press site out there the most, we need to help each other, every sale off the site cuts out the middle man and keeps the company going so we can afford advertising, and it helps your fellow DMP authors get known, in turn they will do it for you! However, some people will only buy from Amazon – either because they have an account with them (Prime members get free shipping and special deals) so they stick to what they like best. To sell yourself to these people there are tips:

Start an Amazon connect account. Do an author profile page on Amazon! Make sure you use professional photo, link to your official site, complete about you (tip – the key words you use will link you through "so you'd like to guides" expertise will drive traffic to your book.) Also check out Amapedia – Amazon's internal wiki, topics will get traffic to you. Write as many book reviews as you can – especially for another author like you with your signature under your name….because if other people like that authors subject clearly they are looking for similar books and will look you up as well. Be kind about that other writer or you will look bad and we don't want that. Use Amazon's 'Listmania feature" – by creating lists of books you like and put one of yours in there too.

Having a great idea is only the first step, though. Ideas are not worth anything until you put them into action.

Putting ideas into action is where many people stumble. They may be afraid to try something new, or confused about how to get started. Or they may think they do not have the skills or resources necessary to make their idea successful.

Here is a simple three step plan for going from idea to action: Make a plan and write it down. A big project is less intimidating when you break it into a series of small steps. If you are not sure where to start, work backwards. For example, if your project is to create and sell a new product online, one of the last steps might be to make sales. What do you have to do before that? You need to have a sales page on a website, a way to accept payments and the product itself. What steps will you have to take to put those things in place? Keep working backwards until you reach the beginning.

If you are not sure what needs to be done, then your first step is to learn. Identify the resources available to teach you what you need to know or the people who can help you.

With authors starting out, you usually have a very a limited marketing budget, but publicity can be done cheap or often free. Read Jay Conrad Levinson's *Guerrilla Marketing* books for tips.

I think it is important to realize that not only does free publicity helps your budget as a starving artist; it also does not mean that it is necessarily lower quality. Self-promotion/free publicity can be much more effective because people are becoming increasingly able to "tune out" advertisements. We skip ads, block them on our electronics or ignore them in magazines and only notice funny billboards. People honestly would rather listen to the author make comments online on their pages or on a radio show, it is a more personal connection, when they identify with you, they will be more inclined to advertise you themselves, and become repeat buyers of your work.

## Press Releases

A press release will not get you quoted on the front page of the *New York Times*. In saying that, however, a press release is a very good marketing tool as it does answer questions reporters have about your new book, and it helps make it so your book shows up on Google searches for your company or product so prospects can find you.

Some of the best places to distribute your press releases are PRWeb.com the internet's leading press release services; PR Web submits releases to a huge network of journalists and bloggers. They also submit releases directly to major search engines and news sites. PRWeb charges a fee for each release, and another called PRLog.com which is free to post your release on the site. All submissions are optimized for search engines, and premium distribution packages are available for a fee.

You also can do a quick Google search and email various e-zines editor to see if it fits with them, once you know the genre you both fit into.

*Blurbs, Forewords, Afterword's, and Reviews*
Collect comments people write about your books, they help you sell if you quote them on your website – and this can be anything someone endorsed you on, no matter if it is written, audio and video testimonials regularly and post them on your web site, include them in your newsletter, add them to your social media page once in a while.

Give it back to others, especially if they have for you. As Zig Zigler said, "You will get all you want in life, if you help enough other people get what they want". Do for others and they will be happy to do so for you in return, at least for the most. Share praise for great products, services and books you enjoy. Providing results-based testimonials is great way of expanding your visibility. Of course, you should only provide testimonials for businesses you honestly feel deserve a raving testimonial. If you wrote only one a month, you'd have 12 other authors promoting you after a year. I have done it on Gene Simmons book to promote Hail Thyself! This also works with video endorsements.

Ask for them! You never know unless you ask if they will say no or not. Seasoned writers will do it on a steady basis because they usually put the title of a book after their name, which helps keep them in sales, it is a quid pro quo. Do not over ask for the favor from the same person or it will be obvious favoritism. Writers know that is how word of mouth spread, celebrity sponsors of products on TV is how companies sell everything. In this case, seek experts in the topic you are writing in.

*Forewords, and Afterword's*
Like press blurbs, having someone known write the forewords (and afterword's) in you books can help immensely. The brand they provide and the fan base they bring with them when they more known author comments on your work can gain you notoriety. Over the years, some of the most noted experts on genres I write about have not only agreed to be contributors, commenter's but they have become collogues or even best friends.

*Book reviews*
Book reviews can make or break you for the most part. Amazon.com, Good Reads are locations you will find your work talked about. Self-esteem a note on reviews. Like a famous actor once mentioned, don't seek out every review – especially the negative ones - and take it personally. Don't bury you head in the sand and live in denial either. If everyone says you need spell check (see editing your books) or you just don't have the chops for being a writer (see rejection) pay attention. That doesn't mean give up, it means try harder. Once you will let it to you down it will stifle your creative flow. Learn from critiques, heed it if it is the advice of those you trust and especially your editor. The same thing applies to Google when you type in your own name. You will find what people are saying about your work and you as a person.

Do not let fear stop you. Do not worry about what other people especially those who would like to see you fail. Consider it sour grapes and push on. Take action every single day, even if it is seems small. Small things add up, like an avalanche, when you stay proactive action on your career, it will make you a success -persistence pays off, and little things do add up.

Now that you have a new book done, you may be considering a sequel or wondering what next topic you should work on. Why not let your fans help you figure that out? Just because you are an expert in your genre, don't lose sight of the fact so is your audience. Smart authors don't just write what they want, they adjust their topics and give the audience what they demand to earn a living. No matter what genre you fit into there are trends within them. Wattpad (the so-called "YouTube of ebooks") can help but more importantly see what is on the bookshelves at stores, on Amazon as new releases and you can stay ahead of the guessing game of what to write next provide what is popular.

*A Literary Agent or no?*
The sad fact of the publishing industry is that there are dubious practices everywhere, one of them is an agent. Remember, it is important to approach agents that deal with the type of book you intend to publish.

There is more to being a writer than just typing words, as you have learned by now. That's where a Literary Agent comes in handy. An agent is the book-marketing expert who can sell your manuscript to publishing professionals, and usually will give your work a fighting chance to be seen above the hundreds that are in the piles of big time publishers. Your job, as the writer is one, to do excellent work and two, locate one that will get you where you need to go.

The WritersNet Directory of Literary Agents may include agents who charge a reading fee for reviewing a manuscript. This is often considered an indicator of a disreputable agent. Agents who charge a reading fee are required to include this fact in their WritersNet profile. Since agents enter themselves into that database, you cannot assume that every literary agent in our directory is reliable or fair.

For advice about a particular agent, or agency, seek writers blogs, forums and ask people who do write professionally – remember, networking. Discussion forums are one of the best locations to inquire. Alternatively, check whether the agent you are considering approaching is a member of the Association of Authors Representatives (US) http://aaronline.org/or the Association of Authors Agents (UK). Both organizations have stringent membership requirements.

Also, take a look at Science Fiction and Fantasy Writers of America, Inc is very useful resource for writers, which describes what writers should beware of and offers warnings regarding untrustworthy agents.

# Your First Public Appearance

Your first public appearance!

A newly published writer, caught up in the excitement of holding your first book or seeing your work reviewed in a publication, seldom realizes that a world of work lies in front of you. I often tell my writers at Dark Moon Press that the real work begins after the book comes out.

As days roll into weeks and months, dreams of a Stephen King or J.K. Rowling-like existence are usually replaced by the harsh reality that the world isn't yet clamoring for your book.

The best bookseller is the author. You know your book better than anyone, and no one has as much riding on its success. By nature, most authors are very intimidated at the thought of pushing their own books but in the highly competitive world of publishing, this is a necessity. Even large companies will tell you that you have to market yourself on social media and get signings and radio interviews. Surprise! It isn't up to the publisher to push your work. The publisher's job is to edit, format, design a cover, and get it printed and off to distributors to make money. It is up to you to make it a bigger success.

This section is going to be lengthy, covering everything from making the contacts to how to prepare and personal appearance. It is critical for success.

*Setting up the signing*
Setting up a book signing as an independent author is difficult but not impossible. When I published my first book, I was actually able to set up two book signings at my local Little Professor Bookstore and

Borders with some ease. Being local helps. Getting massive amounts of them in order to do a nationwide tour is much more complex.

All I did was walk in with a copy of my book, asked to speak with a manager, and we set up the signing on the spot.

Unfortunately, a lot of chain book stores have gone out of business. The only major brand book stores left, it seems, are Barnes & Noble and Half Priced Books. B&N rarely will allow independent authors to do book signings unless their warehouse already has the books in stock.

The process of getting your books into Barnes & Noble can be done if you print your books on www.lulu.com.

It's actually not as important to host book signings, nowadays, as it is to market your book, due to the fact that social media can reach out to a much larger audience than ever before. However it's still a fulfilling experience that can give authors exposure and interaction with buyers and potential readers and help you to feel more comfortable "pitching" the book to complete strangers. I have another huge section just on speaking and if you want to be an educator/motivational speaker in our next tutorial.

*Location: Think of Someplace Different*
If you're an author, consider either an independent book store, a coffee house, or a restaurant with an interior decor that would match the feel you want from a book signing.

*Libraries*
Public libraries often sponsor author appearances and can be one of your best sources for finding speaking engagements. Face-to-face meetings are most effective. Go boldly in, book in hand, and describe to the librarians your purpose and background. Visit your area libraries and, when you travel out of town, introduce yourself at libraries there as well. Librarians are wonderful resources. Give them your business card and a simple pamphlet outlining your fee, your preferences on group size and ages, and a short description of your presentation. This isn't the time for

humility. You've written a book, a feat most people consider impressive enough. Few of your potential listeners will ever guess how insecure you feel.

## Get Attention Ahead of Time

Just because you set up an event, it doesn't mean people will come! You have to announce it to as many people as possible.

In the weeks leading up to the book signing, I announced the event everywhere I could (Facebook, Twitter, Instagram). Things have changed and made it very easy to get public attention compared to when I first started out. I have a huge section on Social Media Marketing in this course. You want to give people plenty of time to plan to come to your event but not so much that they forget about it.

If you have put together a press release you can compile a list of local media ahead of time and send it out about a month before the signing. Don't expect any media coverage, especially if you're not well known and the book signing is held in an atypical place.

## Book Store Signings

If you are like me, you seclude yourself away from the world in your home office feverishly working on your newest book. From the moment you can say your new book is done (and before beginning several others) you are ready to meet the world for book signings in order to connect with your fans who enjoy reading your work, and you hope, sell books to them. Sometimes a fan will bring a new person with them and introduce them to your material. When approaching a bookstore, or other venue, about a book signing approach them at least several months in advance. Ask for their public relations person or, if they don't have one, the store manager.

Bookstores generally set their in-store event calendar a few months in advance. Many venues book even earlier to ensure they are able to list the event in their calendar, etc.

Begin gathering reviews and blurbs to add to your press releases and/or website. A collection of reviews and reader comments is motivational and sometimes necessary to capture the interest of some bookstore managers. It helps the hosts of your signings to create flyers for the event as well.

Develop a city by city (or store by store in your local area if you are want to start smaller) strategy. From the Internet, gather names, addresses, and phone numbers of stores you believe would be receptive to your book. The chains have bookstore locator searches you can use to locate stores in your targeted areas and will provide all needed information. Prepare a checklist to follow when you contact them. Call the store, or, if local, go into the store in person and ask to speak to the manager (or public relations). Email is a good follow-up tool, but do not rely on it to nail down business. Tell him/her that you are a local author and that you would like to make sure your book is in their system and, possibly, set up a signing.

Note: Never assume. Check first by looking for your book via a search on that chain's website, if possible, to make sure it is now appearing in their database so that you are well armed when approaching them.

Tell the manager you would like to arrange a book signing and provide your ISBN. Taking a copy of the book along is helpful. He or she will look the number up, usually at that very moment, to verify that they can order it. They usually will then offer to set up a signing (have your calendar in front of you when you call or go in) or will direct you to their in-house worker in charge of publicity and events.

Offer to email or send, via snail mail, information about your book that the store can use for publicity purposes. This information should include a flyer/advertisement about the book, a short author's bio, any reviews/reader responses you have, and a small photo of yourself. I contacted a Community Relations Manager (CRM) at Barnes & Noble recently and she told me, in no uncertain terms, if an author doesn't know their book's ISBN, or worse if an author doesn't even know what an ISBN is, she's not interested in working with that author. Be prepared to deliver a complimentary review copy for the decision-maker. Don't be stingy…this is worth it!

*Why a book event would be good for the store and its customers and how the store can procure copies for the proposed event*

This is important as stores like doing business through their normal channels, and that typically means sourcing through one of their preferred distributors like Ingram, Baker & Taylor, or Partners Book Distributing. Stores aren't generally interested in sourcing books either directly from you or from your publisher (if you have one). If your book is only available as a non-returnable, print-on-demand title, a book event is practically impossible in the big chain stores.

Stores are open to the idea of signings by POD authors because they DO generate store traffic. If they're not interested in signings, the manager is new or deluded and out of touch about the book business anyway. Call back in a few months. More than likely a new manager will be working there who will be more open to the idea.

Barnes & Noble, Books-a-Million, Costco, and other national retailers routinely host authors published by large traditional publishing houses as well as self-published authors. Such book-related events are part of the overall business strategy at bookstores, warehouse clubs, grocery stores, airport concessionaires, and other outlets. I will have a full contact PDF for you of information on how to reach these chain stores as a bonus for the course!

Unless the store provides it, bring an easel and a large poster of you and your book to the signing. I also bring a small letter-size ad that I slip into a plastic sheet/picture frame. (You can find these at Wal-Mart for a couple of bucks.) Generally the store will place you and your books in a high-traffic area at a table or stand with your books stacked on it.

If they're smart, they will display your book at checkout registers as well. If they haven't thought of doing this, ask them if it is possible.

After the signing, sign any leftover books. Take a photo or two of the signing and offer to write up an article on the manager's behalf for their trade magazine. This is a win/win situation if you can make this happen.

As for the day of the event I know you wonder what's expected of you. Simple. Follow the guidelines established by your host store. They've held many signings before yours, and have a system in place. Trust me, if you ever want to be invited back, you must get with the program. That means create a poster exactly like they want, offer a giveaway (like a bookmark) that falls within their guidelines, and stick to your allotted timeslot. If you're not sure about something you've planned, always ask in advance. Most signings last for two hours.

*Print books early!*

Make sure your books are arriving on time for the author appearance. Don't laugh. Many an author has been disappointed by a carton of books not showing up until after they had the event. Check and double check that your books are arriving. Get tracking information and stay close in touch with the publishing and bookselling staff members who are responsible, like the publicist and the bookstore manager or bookstore's event coordinator.

People who show up do not always come to buy, however. Always figure half those invited will actually show, and those who do will not buy. Sound disheartening? I would rather tell you the truth than lie and have you find out later and be bitter. Better to know the averages ahead and be happy you get a quarter of the invites as buyers. Some people like to stop by just to say hello and tell you that they enjoy your books, or just to meet you at all. Others will be there just to stop by to ask questions and bring up different aspects of your work they have read in order to get resolution directly from you, the author. Sometimes you will find there is someone in the audience who is an aspiring author, someone who dreams of being published. They go for two reasons primarily. First, they inquire about what it's really like to be a writer. Second, they hope you will impart wisdom to them on how to get started, how to follow in your footsteps. Not every person that comes up to you during the signing will buy the book. Don't be desperate and try to force a sale to everyone you talk to, but definitely show your enthusiasm and confidence in your own work. Enjoy the experience of talking to people.

*Be Prepared*

Always be prepared when you go to the venue. Have a good supply of swag/giveaway items such as business cards, bookmarks, postcards, etc. showcasing your book cover and where it can be purchased. Plenty of places make them cheap but high quality, such as www.got-print.net. Just make sure you have your cover picture at 300 dpi resolution or it will look distorted and unprofessional.

Know ahead what you are going to say and how you want to emphasize, by tone or expression. Consider this an act, and you are in command of the audience's attention. Do not commit the flaw most students in school do and read your speech verbatim from your papers! Focus on the key points, use note cards for dates, a few words for the concept as an overall to nudge your brain. Keep pens with you, for autographing copies. Sharpies are the standard for many authors. Thick or thin — your preference. But have plenty on hand.

*Bring your book's promotional materials*

If you're signing at a large event where many other authors are signing as well, it's great to have bookmarks or other promotional items with you at your table to bring some of the reading public to you. Be sure to bring relevant promotional items such as bookmarks and pens to give away to your audience. Add a headshot to an unpublished short story or excerpt from a new piece, sign it and offer a free sneak peek into your upcoming work. Have a drawing for a tote bag with your autographed book inside. Any small item is a reminder of the event and helps sell you to them after you are gone and they pick up the object later, as days go by, and they remember how they enjoyed meeting you.

An Opt-In list can be very useful in future marketing for your next book! Place a sign-in sheet or guest book on your table where your audience may provide their information and email addresses to receive special promotions and upcoming information. This builds your fan base so people remember you later. Get people to follow you on social media is very helpful, I have gained dozens of friend requests or followers during speaking events by simply asking.

Follow up. Donate a copy of your book to the location of your book signing. If they are going to purchase copies to sell, offer to sign those as well. Remember to send a thank you to everyone involved; the event location for hosting your signing, the opt-in audience for attending, and any press (reporters, photographers, etc.) that contributed to news regarding your event.

Ask a friend to help assist you. Hopefully you and the location staff will be busy with customers, but remember they are in business to sell to other customers, not hold your hand. You are a guest to drive traffic to them. A friend or family member acting as your assistant will help to keep a professional flow. Your assistant can hand out bookmarks and freebies, replenish your books when they get low, ask customers to join the mailing list, make announcements to invite customers to the table, and take pictures of the event for future promotional use.

Get to know the audience. Mingle before your talk and pay attention to what type of people are in your audience. Get a feel for how they think and tailor what you say to them. In the very least you will feel less uneasy since the familiarity will be more like old friends talking.

It's also going to be awkward and uncomfortable at times when people look at you and you're standing there by yourself waiting for someone to come up and talk. Smile and do your best to be at ease. Body language is everything. Show confidence even if you may not feel it at that moment. It will go a long way in making you look intelligent, knowledgeable, and professional to your audience.

It's also helpful if you invite friends or family to keep you company during the dull moments and give you a boost of encouragement. They can also take payments on your phone app like PayPal or Strip, and another to film/take photos for your social media in order to show off how successful it went to those who missed out. They can fill out the audience in case you don't have as many people as you would like. This makes you look in demand.

I also use the trick of having a plant, that is, someone I know in the audience. Someone who will start asking questions since no one likes to be the first to do so. It encourages others in the audience, who don't know you, to go ahead and ask questions they may have also.

In the old days, you didn't have social media as a way to get noticed by fans. It was strictly newspaper reviews, trade fairs, or magazines doing an article or making an event at your local book store.

With a great book and a concerted local marketing plan, your book can gain national momentum and you can be in-demand throughout the country. But first, let's cover the aspects of how you look for the big day.

*How to dress*
They say never judge a book by its cover but we do. You've picked up probably about every book and, at least to some subconscious level, by your impression in the wording of the title, or the art on the cover, you were drawn to it. We are a superficial lot and have our likes pretty well developed at a young age. Appearance is the first thing others judge us on because we see an individual from a distance and make a judgment call about them before they ever come near us. By now you may see yourself as polished on the inside but your outer appearance needs examining as best as you can, because no matter how you've changed your thinking, we are visual creatures and our first impression is what lasts the longest. If you want to have people listen to your words, you must first capture their attention.

*Ritual of Routine*
Human beings are creatures of habit. Bear this in mind when realizing you wish to improve. People get into the habit of doing things all the time. Bad choices, lack of paying attention to details can be reversed

only if we are acutely conscious of the fact that we do it. We can change these things with effort and how we take care of ourselves should be the next move. Remember, once you are in the public eye as an author, you will get noticed so take care in how you dress, act, and groom yourself. I have been stopped in grocery stores late at night, in movie theaters, and in hotels because people wanted to meet me and get an autograph,

## Hygiene, simple but critical

As if this was not an expected aspect of gaining a better life, I don't know what would be more critical! How we work on making ourselves more presentable can unlock many doors.

### Nails

Women in particular notice two things about guys; their shoes and their nails. Both show care and concern for the little details of proper grooming. A man who will go the extra mile to pay attention to the small things will do the same for them.

### Hair

A disheveled and/or greasy head of hair is an obvious sign of someone not caring about their looks. An eccentric cut or coloring (unless it is a music or artistic profession that might benefit from it) and one's skin are similar in how we are perceived. Our perceptions are visual first and foremost because we see people before they speak or any other primary senses we use. However, another way to manipulate and influence things in your favor come from a more subtle form and that is by smell.

### Scent

It has been proven that certain smells influence people's moods and affect their work performance through associated and conditioned responses. The smell of vanilla can trigger a memory of Mom baking in the kitchen. Smelling rosemary while studying for a test can help you remember what you studied better than without it. Using a diffuser necklace with lavender oil in it can calm you down before a stressful presentation.

The use of scent to entice others has been around for thousands of years. Incense was used for religious purposes by the Egyptians, who believed that they could communicate with the gods by raising scented smoke. This is how we started using the word perfume - per fumum, which is Latin for "through smoke". Myrrh, frankincense, peppermint, and rose were common ingredients in early perfumes. The Egyptians also invented glass and used glass perfume bottles to store their perfumes. Cleopatra used the smell of rose petals to enhance the emotions of the love of her followers.

The Persians were the ones who perfected the art of preserving scents; while Alexander the Great brought perfume to Greece after invading Egypt. With the increases in chemistry to create synthetic ingredients to enhance our attractiveness, this naturally continued and became less expensive.

People are vain and have perpetuated wearing perfume and cologne as well as scented soaps and, later, body washes, as part of hygiene in our modern society. As for myself, I stick with Aspen, it goes very well with Fresh deodorant, and Irish Spring Body Wash combined. People often fail to realize, even an expensive body scent can be bad on you as we each have our own chemical reaction to the things we put on our bodies. What smells good on one person may not on you, so test it on your wrist, blow on the skin, and wait a moment before you smell the area. Also, try not to use too much or too strong of a scent as, even though it may smell good, too strong of a scent can cause negative reactions in those with allergies or breathing issues.

When I started adding to the new book on success, I nearly didn't add to the chapter on attire and improvement. That would have been a big mistake. After doing more study I located a lot more on the subject that I am happy to share, from the psychological study of changing your appearance effectively to a deeper look at how it makes others see you. I also will be sharing tips and a few exercises you can do to make the changes more effective.

The effects wardrobe has on others is a very powerful thing. There is a reason people call a suit a 'power suit'. It is the uniform of the successful man (and often woman). Lawyers, business tycoons, and other professionals dress to impress and pay plenty to look as powerful as they are. I've always said I will know when I am a huge hit when I can afford an Armani. Dress like a king and you will be treated like one. People fail to realize that what you wear will affect your outlook, how you see yourself in the mirror, and that adds to self-esteem. People will look at you through different eyes and the resulting compliments help also.

*Science of 'Dress for Success'*
"Dressing for success may sound intimidating, expensive, and a bit vain; however, keep in mind that your presentation creates credibility," says author Michelle Moore

In 2012 a study from Northwestern University created a new term "enclothed cognition" which was to illustrate the psychological effect clothing has on its wearer. Researchers found people who wear nicer clothing are prone to perform better academically. There is actually some credence to the old "dress for success" mantra. I am admittedly old fashioned. I grew up in an era left over by grandparents who dressed in their Sunday best going to church. From a very young age I actually enjoyed how I felt in a dress shirt, slacks, and suit coat, and I do to this day. Every time you go out, you reflect an image that tells others how to treat you. They are sizing you up and making an assumption of what you do for a living, your income level, and your current level of success in life, based solely on your appearance. Successful people like to maintain an impeccable image. Why? Because they know that their image is part of their brand. Your image is an outside indicator of who you are as a person. A big part of advancing in life is looking the part. A keen sense of style can lead to greater opportunities and higher levels of success. I feel this is important and that it builds confidence when you project it. Others who see you typically think you are somebody because you dress like it. The old advice to dress for the job you want, not the job you have, may have roots in more than simply how others perceive you. Many studies show that the clothes you wear can affect your mental and physical performance. There is a growing body of research that suggests there is something biological happening when we put on a snazzy outfit and feel like a new person.

In August 2015 Social Psychological and Personality Science, a unique short reports journal in social and personality psychology, asked subjects to change into formal or casual clothing before cognitive tests. Wearing formal business attire increased abstract thinking, which is an important aspect of creativity and long-term strategizing. The experiments suggest the effect is related to feelings of power. I believe the decline of people having standards, being lazy, and a lax society is to blame. I remember many times, in college, being asked if I was a professor, as I wore a suit and tie to class. I was appalled at seeing how everyone else came into school; lounge pants, ratty t-shirts, etc. It was a career based higher learning institution for paralegals, CNA's, and business majors! Professionalism was (and is everywhere) sorely lacking. I say bring back the good old days when people looked and acted like ladies and gentlemen.

"Whether you like it or not, your appearance is the first thing people notice about you--and first impressions are usually formed within the first 30 seconds," says Brenda Ferguson Hodges, a California-based image consultant, and career coach. "Appearance affects hiring decisions and plays a major role. Hiring managers need to be able to visualize you in that position they are trying to fill."

Nicole Williams, the best-selling author, agrees. "On a job interview, your attire makes a statement about yourself before you even open your mouth," she says. "A scuffed shoe, a messy bag, or a low cut shirt can speak volumes. You need to wear your 'power outfit.' Have a favorite skirt that always makes you feel great when you wear it? Why not pair that with a blazer? It's okay to show off your personality through your clothes, as long as you aren't wearing a lime green mini skirt. Stick to business-professional looks."

## Manipulation through Color

Color is another less often used tool in the arsenal of getting what you want in life. When it comes to color and psychology, researchers have explored the effects of color on mood and behavior. Frank Mahnke discusses in his book *Color, Environment, and Human Response*, how color has a vibration, like music. Artists understand the power of color to manipulate the viewers of their work to evoke a feeling. Color has an impact on people in many ways, both psychologically and physically – with emotional, physiological, and psychological effects. To manage the impression you give, change the way you are perceived, and let others to see the positive attributes you have by changing their initial impression of you. Once you understand the power of color brings out desired reactions, the emotional effects of color can be used to your advantage in everyday life, it can even create the image you desire.

Color influences your brain, nervous system, and hormonal activity. For instance, if you sat in an entirely red room, your pulse and blood pressure would increase. This was used in brothels in the old days and has also influenced the nickname "whore red" for said color of lipstick. This effect can also be seen at funerals, or in court, as people tend to naturally react more formal towards a person in black as it is the color of authority. As such we associate it with the respect that we offer those in the robes of judges, clergy, and, at times, the uniforms of law enforcement officers.

Personally I use black as a personal expression. I was jokingly referred to as 'the man in black" for years, when I worked at a clothing store. I had first chance at selecting the best of the shipment and with my discount, took advantage of it. Black is classic, used often with tuxedoes and a staple of wardrobe for the Victorian period. It denotes sophistication, power, elegance, and mystery. Strength of colors combined are even more powerful still than being separate. I combine my black suits with shirts of burgundy or amethyst; other colors that convey what I'm trying to put out there. I also mix my accessories to emphasize the feeling with silver, when it comes to my watch, cufflinks, tie clips, and sunglass frames. Black along with silver (or gold, if you prefer) evoke prestige and luxury which helps create the impression of prosperity and economic success. By creating the illusion, and following it, you will create that prosperity and success. Part of it is in the image in the minds of others, and within you. When you look in the mirror and feel more powerful you will act that way.

Using the opposite end of the color wheel you can induce a calming effect. At times, you may wish to appear friendly and approachable, by wearing earth tones, such as brown, which are stable, grounding, or grey which is neutral and calm. According to color psychology, grey can also be boring and conservative. White represents clarity, innocence, cleanliness, spirituality, purity, hope; as seen in robes worn by the Pope. It can also be sterile and detached, as it is the traditional color worn by physicians.

Tan come across as warm, and more approachable. Want sympathy in court or to appear more solid at a job interview? Wear calming and non-threatening colors like green or blues. Blue and green are very calming. Blue often characterizes dependability, trustworthiness, and security. Green represents growth and stimulates possibility. It is calming, soothing, and its relaxing feeling is associated with healing and nature. Yellow is very happy, warm, and stimulating, whereas purple represents nobility and dignity, and is the color related to higher intellect.

For attracting attention use more loud colors such as reds, oranges, or yellows. The color red, as stated earlier, is associated with everything from lip stain back to ancient civilization (think whores of Babylon) for enticing men for sex. In nature, the bottom of a female baboon becomes redder in appearance to attract the males in much the same way. When blood rushes to parts of the body, the genitals specifically, it does the same. Red actually stimulates your pituitary gland and causes the release of the hormone epinephrine. Your body sends out an increase in pulse rate, blood pressure, and also the circulation of adrenaline. The color red increasing breathing and raises emotion. This biological response causes the human mind to connect red to passionate feelings. This is why Valentine's Day cards and red roses have more of an impact on the recipient than just making money for Hallmark and Russell-Stovers! Psychology suggests that red is the most dominant and stimulating, passionate, exciting, and powerful of colors.

Color psychology can be a simple yet effective way to enhance your image. It carries over to room decorating, creating subtle but effective impact on how people may respond to you. Advertisers use color psychology. Most often, people will not even know they are being guided to a particular feeling or thinking pattern.

"Your appearance not only shows that you're taking the opportunity seriously, that you are eager to make a good impression, and that you'd fit in nicely within the corporate culture; it can also communicate that you have respect for the interviewer," says Mark Strong, a life, career, and executive coach based in New York.

*Communicating your message*
Articulation and pronunciation are important. People not only judge you by how you look but also by what you say and how you say it. A Articulation shows that you pay attention to the nuances of speaking, and that educational standards have been met when it comes to your pronunciation of words. People who use slang, Ebonics, and "text" talk in daily life – even on school papers, one of my former professors informed me – are never going to command respect. They will be looked upon as ghetto or trailer trash, and deservedly so.

Language - knowing what to say and how, proper pronunciation and articulation - separates you in the mind of your listener, your reader, and your interviewer, from the rabble. People skills are also important. When you sit in front of someone while looking for a job or being interviewed for a promotion, they're judging you as much as your résumé. Who you are, how you act, what you look like. Remember, if you don't impress them, there are thousands more equally qualified people ready and willing to take your place. It is a dog-eat-dog world and never forget it.

It may seem like a given but being a successful author also means paying attention to how you look to your fans.

Once you know what your customers want, create it for them, which is why I started to record videos of myself at events, and, I not only have a YouTube channel, but I also frequently add the videos to my website.

I realized not everyone can get out to the events and hear me speak, either due to the costs, time off work, or things that come up in life. I have a friend who does camerawork for me at large events, and acts as personal assistant and driver, so it frees me up to focus on my speeches, and it sure doesn't hurt having the company and the help with carrying books, which do get heavy in quantity.

*Self-Critique, Reflecting back*
Thank your fans, they appreciate it! Remember, everyone wants to be appreciated and your fans who keep buying from you have helped pay your bills! So be grateful back. Thank everyone involved in the appearance at the store, library, event, or where ever you spoke at.

Make sure to write notes to your bookstore or event "host." It takes a lot of effort to mount these sorts of events and your thanks will be much appreciated. Plus, it will help you get fondly remembered when your next book is published.

# Public Speaking

When it comes to our fears, as people, the two highest on the list are dying and public speaking.

I remember back in college when I took a Public Speaking class and was probably the only one not terrified to do a lecture in front of the class. At that point in my career, I had already done a speech at Indiana-Purdue University of Fort Wayne as a guest at a world religions seminar, which consisted of me and several church, and other religious organizations, elders, in front of three hundred students and faculty. So I suppose it is a matter of perspective. I did utilize a great number of the class's concepts that I added to my personal experience, and I will share them here.

Remember to relax before your events. It is very important to clear your mind and decompress after your speaking engagement as well. If you are nervous it will show to your audience. As time passes and you do more and more events, you will gain more confidence (with experience and knowing your subject). You have to listen to the people in the audience who are close to you, that you trust, to tell you how you did. You need to project your voice some you can be heard, nobody likes to strain to hear you. I am guilty of this, even years later, but having been made aware of it I try more. This also boosts confidence, in the listener, that you are an impassioned speaker. Remember if YOU care, they will too!

Public speaking and fear

You can indeed conquer the fear of public speaking. It can be done. In years past I was a shy, quiet introvert, afraid to speak to a group, let alone a room full of people or on television, yet I evolved. Talk to friendly faces. Find the people you met earlier and look at a few of them while you speak and come back to them as you gaze around the room. People like it when they feel you are talking to them, it makes them feel special.

Don't open with a joke. Most of us are not funny and it will sound lame, so don't start off making them feel awkward for you.

Don't announce that you are nervous. The audience doesn't necessarily know that you are. They assume you are the expert since you wrote the book; they are present just to learn what you know. Don't bring it to their attention. Remember that the audience is investing their time and attention on you.

Smile. You will feel more relaxed and confident with a smile, and it will warm up the room to you. If you are too uncomfortable to make eye contact with people, just look slightly above the heads in the audience. They won't know the difference. However, be careful to notice movement as someone may be signaling you with a question.

Don't fret so much about any mistakes you make or if you forget what you had in mind to say, you can always touch on it later as if it were on purpose. Stop worrying and take a deep breath. You know your material. You are the one who wrote it after all. So many times I used to print out tons of notes, even the entire book. I highlighted and scribbled notes in it, only to find that I barely glanced at it all and didn't cover half of what I wanted to say even though, going in, I worried I would talk too fast and run out of things to say. That never happens for me.

Know how you want to wrap your lecture. Close with a brief message that you want the audience to remember, make it leave them in awe of the entire point of the speech. It makes them forget any mistakes you might have made during the middle.

Look for opportunities to speak in front of groups whenever you can. You might want to start with small groups and work up to bigger and bigger ones, but practice whenever you can until it becomes second nature.

Get honest feedback from others. Many years ago I was in a training program for speakers where we evaluated each other. After a presentation, each person in the class would tell the speaker one thing they had done well and one thing they could do better next time. Ask someone you trust and respect to do that for you. Constructive criticism makes you better if you accept it and use it for improvement. At some events you go to, the audience is encouraged to fill out comment cards.

This is done for the event's benefit and helps you get invited back, provided they liked your speech that is. I always read critiques that get submitted after conventions if the head of programming sends the document to me.

Critique yourself. After you have been speaking for a while, go back and listen to a recording (or watch a video) of one of your early presentations. This is another reason why I video myself at events, in part for advertising online and on my website to show others how well I know my material, but also to critique myself. How did I look? How was my posture? Did I smile enough, or too much? Did I wear the right thing for the nature of the event I was at? You will be amazed at how much your speaking skills will have improved, as well as your relaxed demeanor.

How successful we are at selling ourselves, our products, and our services depend on our ability to stand up and be heard. What often prevents us from telling our story successfully is not our inability to articulate what we do or how strongly we believe in the value of what we offer. Instead, it is simply the fear of speaking in front of an audience. Being nervous while presenting can put a dent in your credibility and have an adverse effect on achieving your business goals.

To manage the fear of speaking in public, you need to first understand the root cause of the fear. One of the best explanations comes from Scott Berkun, in *Confessions of a Public Speaker*. "The design of the brain's wiring—given its long operational history, hundreds of thousands years older than the history of public speaking makes it impossible to stop fearing what it knows is the worst tactical position for a person to be in," Berkun says. That "worst tactical position" is standing alone, in an open place, with no place to hide, without a weapon, facing a large group of creatures staring at you. As Berkun puts it, being in this situation "meant the odds were high that you would soon be attacked and eaten alive ... Our ancestors, the ones who survived, developed a fear response to these situations."

Understanding that our brain can't tell the difference between a real threat (a pack of wolves about to attack you) and an imagined threat (a group of your peers watching you present) is the first step to overcoming the fear. This awareness can help you manage the "false alarm" that happens in the absence of real danger. As you feel your heart racing when you first start your presentation, you can consciously and deliberately interrupt the fear response with a quick deep breath and a rational thought, "This is just a false alarm." The more you get into the habit of interrupting the fear response as soon as you feel it happening, the quicker you'll prevent it from being your default response every time you present in front of a group. You must ingrain in your mind the thought that the fear of public speaking is simply a misfiring of the caveman "fight or flight" fear response, and that you can overcome this.

Here are 11 practical tips to help you manage performance anxiety so you can focus on your key messages, as detailed by Bruna Martinuzzi, President and Founder, Clarion Enterprises Ltd.

1. Reframe the questions you ask yourself. When you worry before a high-stakes presentation, you may have a tendency to ask yourself negative questions, such as "What will happen if I forget my material?" This form of self-talk is like throwing gasoline in a room on fire. All it does is heighten your anxiety. Replace these negative questions with positive ones. Give this a try; it will calm the noise in your head.

2. Practice as if you're the worst. When you know your material well, there's a tendency to get sloppy when practicing a speech: You might flip through the slides, mentally thinking about what you are going to say, without actually rehearsing out loud exactly what you plan to say. This results in a presentation that's not as sharp as it could be and might cause you to be nervous once you have 100 pairs of eyes staring at you. You can also forget some important sub-points and key soundbites.

3. Avoid this by practicing out loud and verbalizing your complete presentation. For a high-stakes presentation, do this at least five times, at spaced intervals, to encode your material in long-term memory. It's also crucial that you practice your transitions—the words that link one idea in your presentation to the next. These are easy to forget if you don't practice them and you end up with a staccato presentation. Transitions are the silken thread that guides your listeners through your story. Some examples: "Now that we have established ..."; "This leads us to ..."

4. Memorize the sequence of your slides. Knowing the sequence of your slides so you can anticipate and announce a slide makes you look in control. Nothing erodes your credibility faster than having to look at a

slide to know what you have to say next. Being perceived as credible boosts your confidence and reduces your anxiety and your fear of failing.

5. Create a backup slide for some answers. One reason people often experience anxiety before a presentation is the fear that they'll be asked questions that might be difficult to answer. Don't get caught off guard. Think carefully of what potential questions might arise and rehearse your best answers. Go one step further by creating slides for some potential questions about complex issues. You can include in your slide important information, numbers, stats or even a pertinent graph or pie chart that would be helpful to the audience. If such a question arises, it's quite okay to say, "I anticipated that you might be asking this question. Let me display a slide that will clearly show ..."

6. Visualize your presentation. A study at Harvard University showed the value of visualization in developing a skill: Two groups of volunteers were presented with a piece of unfamiliar piano music. One group was given a keyboard and told to practice. The other group was instructed to just read the music and imagine playing it. When their brain activity was examined, both groups showed expansion in the motor cortex, even though the second group had never touched a keyboard. Visualization is a powerful mental rehearsal tool that peak sports performers use regularly. Einstein, who's credited with saying that "imagination is more important than knowledge," used visualization throughout his entire life. Take advantage of this tool and visualize yourself successfully delivering your presentation. Concentrate on all the positives of your presentation, and visualize the talk, in detail, from your introduction to your conclusion.

7. Stop seeing your presentation as a performance. Instead, as Jerry Weissman puts it, "treat every presentation as a series of person-to-person conversations." The more you remind yourself of this, the more you can shift your focus away from the fear-inducing thought that you are required to perform.

8. Take some deep breaths. This simple advice cannot be emphasized enough. When you're nervous, you breathe rapidly and shallowly. This is telegraphing to the audience that you're not confident. Slow and measured breathing is a sign that you're in control. Before you go to the

front of the room, concentrate on taking a few, slow breaths. Repeat this a few times. When you start to speak, remember to pause and breathe after you make a point. Psychiatrist Fritz Perls said it powerfully: "Fear is excitement without the breath."

9. Try "power posing" before the presentation. Harvard Business School Professor Amy Cuddy discovered that simply holding our body in an expansive pose for as little as two minutes results in a higher level of testosterone in our body. Testosterone is the hormone linked to power in both animals and humans. At the same time, the expansive pose lowers our level of cortisol, the stress hormone. In her TED video presentation, Cuddy shows a number of expansive poses, such as spreading your legs, placing your hands on your hips, or striking the CEO pose: legs resting on desk, and arms behind your head. You can apply this advice before a presentation to lower your stress level and give yourself a boost. Instead of hunching over your notes or BlackBerry, find a spot where you can have some privacy and adopt an expansive pose: Make yourself as big as you can by stretching your arms out and spreading your legs, or stand on your tiptoes with your hands in the air.

10. Pause frequently. In *The King's Speech*, a movie about the true story of King George VI, one of the successful strategies the speech therapist uses to help the king overcome his stuttering is the use of pauses. Pausing helped the king regain his composure whenever he was gripped by anxiety. When you feel anxious while presenting, consider pausing more frequently. A few strategic pauses between points have a calming effect.

11. Come to terms with audience expressions. Your anxiety level is increased when you misinterpret the audience's facial expression. In normal conversation, we're accustomed to getting feedback from the listener—a nod or a smile here and there that signal approval. But when we present, audiences listen differently. They're more likely to give the speaker a blank stare, which doesn't mean they don't like what they hear; more often than not, it simply means they're concentrating on the message. This is especially true of audience members who are introverted.

I also found other tips from speakers:

## Get Organized

When you organize all of your thoughts and materials it helps you to become much more relaxed and calm. When you have clear, organized thoughts it can greatly reduce your speaking anxiety because you can better focus on the one thing at hand, giving a great speech.

## Practice and Prepare Extensively

Nothing takes the place of practicing and preparing for your speech. Write out a script of your key points, but don't read the script word for word. Prepare for your speech so well that you could answer any possible question thrown at you. Another thing, for some people, as long as you are very comfortable with your material, you can wing it. I find after time I am much smoother with free flow and tossing my stack of notes aside. However, it has to be a topic you know by heart.

## Eliminate Fear of Rejection

"What if my audience hates my speech? What if they boo me off stage?" Try to eliminate all of your fears of rejection. The audience is there to listen to you for a reason.

## Watch Yourself in the Mirror

Practice your speech in front of the mirror as if you were speaking directly to someone. This is also true of watching a video of yourself after the fact. Record your speech on your phone or video camera. Record yourself giving the talk from beginning to end. Then listen to it, or watch it, and make notes on how you could make it better. Some people do not like listening to the sound of their own voice on tape, so it is important that you get used to your own voice and speaking style.

Pay attention to your facial expressions, gestures, and body movements. Do you have a calm demeanor when you speak? If you do, you will be more welcoming to your audience. How do you think you did? Are there areas you think you could have improved? Did you seem stiff or make any weird facial expressions? Did you use "um" often?

Write everything down. Keep practicing and improving. In time you will banish your fears of public speaking.

When you focus on your breathing, your voice will have more resonance and you will relax. Breathe calmly and focus on getting into a rhythm.

There are plenty of people you can practice on. Be sure to tell the person to be completely honest with you in their critique. Speaking directly to another person will help relax you and give you experience with getting feedback from someone. If they have questions about your speech, it is likely that members of an audience will have the same questions.

*PowerPoint Can Be Really Great, Or Really Bad*

Sometimes, having a PowerPoint can be your best friend. It can help you if you lose your train of thought, keep your audience engaged, and give people a good place to grab notes and main points from.

However, do not put paragraphs on one slide.

Read *Eloquence in Public Speaking* by Dr. Kenneth McFarland, whose central message was that the key to eloquence is the emotional component that the speaker brings to the subject.

*Focus On The Material, Not The Audience.*

Focus on delivering your material in the best way possible. Don't worry about audience reactions.

The biggest tip of all? Relax.

When you let go of your stress and relax it eases your body and makes you less tense.

*Don't Overthink Audience Reactions*

There is always going to be someone in the audience on their phone or yawning. Remember that there will always be people who are bored or tired. None of these audience reactions have anything to do with you personally.

*The Typical Compensation for a Public Speaking Event*

Public speaking can be a great source of income. Motivational speaking in and of itself is a profession. I looked into this when my book *Unlocking the Secrets of Control, Wealth, and Power* (this is a course I offer as well!) was released.

*Ways to Make Money from Public Speaking*

Professional Speaking and Motivational Speaking are the two most common aspects of making a living from talking to lots of people, and it is a great side aspect of being a writer that I strongly encourage.

After you perfect the skill of public speaking you may want to do it even more often and get paid for it. Because of this, your books, whatever the topic they focus on, are just a calling card for your expert status and more sales!

You've just been introduced, the crowd is clapping, and you're heading up to the podium. For hours, the audience has been PowerPointed to death, and now it's nearly lunch. You've only got a moment to make an impression. How do you capture your audience?

Be specific sooner. No one is rooting for you to fail. The audience wants to be edified and entertained.

Public speaking is something that is either incredibly terrifying or incredibly fascinating to most people. Being in front of a group of people doing a presentation can be an incredible rush.

Speaking is a great way to grow your audience or platform. It's a powerful medium to share an idea or concept. It's an incredible tool for building a career. Which leads to still more questions.

How do I actually get booked (and preferably paid) to speak? Well, that greatly depends on your potential audience.

*Who do you want to speak to?*

If you could talk to any audience, who would it be? What is the group of people that gets you excited to speak to? Teenagers? Entrepreneurs? Executives? It is all subjective to what you write about in your book. Speak on what you know best.

*What do you want to speak about?*

So let's assume you could speak to that ideal audience. What would you say? What would you want to share with them that will enrich their lives, businesses, etc?

*What makes you qualified to present on this subject?*

Just like writing a book, people will be asking this question of you. Of all the other speakers on the planet who could present on this topic, why you? Perhaps you have a degree on the subject. Maybe you have significant experience. Maybe you have produced serious results with what you want to share. But in this case, being an author in the first place does automatically lend you credibility as an expert in that field, now you just have to prove it to them!

People will ask you what your story is. What they were really asking was, "What was the tragic life event you had to overcome that makes you qualified to motivate us today?"

There's value in just being a really good speaker or being able to eloquently talk about a topic.

Website

In this day and age, a website is your business card. If you're serious about being a writer and especially combining it with speaking, you must have a website. If someone is considering hiring you to speak, they will want to do their homework on you and your website is where they will do it. It doesn't need to be complicated or fancy. Just a page to tell how you are, what you talk about, any recommendations or testimonials and a contact page. Really that's about it, keep it simple so they get it right away.

If you already have a website, then you're a step ahead. Just make sure your site communicates that you're available as a speaker. People won't think to book you as a speaker if they don't know you are one. If someone you know was looking for a speaker, would they think of you? Not because of how good or not good you may be, but do they even know speaking is something you offer?

*Demo Video*

Think of a demo video like a movie trailer. You take a 90-minute movie and boil it down to two and a half minutes of the best stuff. That's exactly what your demo video needs to be. It's just a few short minutes showing highlights from your talk. Just like your website, a demo video is a must. You can tell a potential client you're really good and that you'd be a good fit for their event, but they'll want to see it for themselves. Testimonials only matter a lot if they are huge names in your field, like Tony Robbins or Jack Canfield in the motivational speaking circuit, vouching for you.

But how do you make a demo video if you don't have any footage of you speaking? Like with anything, you start with what you've got. Do you have any speaking engagements coming up? Even just a small workshop or school presentation will work. You just need footage of you speaking.

Alright, so at this point, we've got our website, demo video, and a few testimonials cobbled together.

Another thing to do is create postcards, business cards, and brochures for yourself to send out or leave at events. It should consist of the same key parts as your website:

A speaker profile sheet is a 1 or 2 page pdf that gives your professional and speaking experience. This should include the same things that your author press sheet details, but with extras:

A brief biography/speaker profile

Media coverage that you've had to date

Information about the 2-5 keynote speeches you offer. Make sure they sound compelling.

A list of recent speaking gigs (paid or unpaid).

A couple of well-phrased client testimonials.

Your speaker headshot (ideally professionally photographed).

Your web links.

Details about any publications, awards, professional bodies, or other impressive info.

Once you have your speaker sheet ready, you can start sending it out to agencies or meeting planners for prospective events that would hold you as a speaker.

Now it's time to get after it and start booking some gigs! After you've identified who you want to speak to and what you want to speak about, here's the next big question to ask…

What are the events/conferences my people go to?

When you start a speaking career, focus on marketing to existing conferences. They've already booked speakers, and it is much easier to get someone to use your service if they're already used to paying for that type of service in the first place.

So where do your people gather? Spend some time on Google using related keywords to find conferences, associations, conventions, or other gatherings of that audience. Pro Tip: Search by the state as well. Here's why that is so important; not only will you discover a whole plethora of other options that exist, but oftentimes, it's much easier to get booked with state, regional, or local conferences than it is with bigger national conferences. So start small in your search.

Once you've identified some possible events, then it's time to find the meeting planner or conference organizer. This is usually on the "about page" or "contact page". Depending on the size of the conference, there may be a bunch of people to choose from or it may be pretty clear who the decision maker is. That's the key, find the decision maker.

Here's where a lot of authors and speakers make a big mistake. Once they find a conference they want to speak at and identify the decision maker, they type out a long email (that will never get read) about how great they are and why that event should book them to speak. Instead, what you want to do is, start a conversation, with a brief email, asking about the conference. Preferably something they can answer with a short reply.

One of the best ways to sell a talk is to pre-sell it. If they reply that they want you to present on that topic, then you can get to work. Now of course, if you throw out a one line topic of a possible presentation, it should be something you can actually present on. For me, speaking on writing, publishing, and self-improvement are tops, but I do others subjects, usually based directly from my books.

Keep your requests short and easy to reply to, then conclude with a clear question that could be answered with a simple yes or no. Easy for the recipient.

I included my speaking website at the bottom. I didn't tell them to go to the site. If they're interested, they'll go on their own, do not imply they are too stupid to click the link. All you're trying to do is build a rapport with the decision maker.

Another idea is to research last year's conference. Who did they have speak? What did they speak on? Do you know any of those speakers? If you're already in that industry, then perhaps you can slyly ask them to speak to the head for you by dropping your name. That's why we network, to get a foot in the door.

All of this is about building a relationship and establishing rapport with the decision maker.

Here are a few more tips as you get started with this...

*Speaking Engagements*

You'll most often speak for free before you speak for a fee.

If you've never really spoken much and you don't have a massive fan base already, there's a good chance you won't get paid the first few times you speak. That's not to say you'll never get paid, but to get your foot in the door, you'll often be speaking for free. Remember, you're trying to build a relationship with the decision maker, so if you can present an insanely good workshop at their conference for free one year, there's a better shot at getting paid the next year. I used that to get in to teach at a couple events and conventions; I volunteered and got to know the people who ran the event and then they asked me to come speak.

*Know what speakers get paid for*

Just because you're an expert on a topic doesn't mean people will pay for it. There are lots of topics that work well as a free workshop but the event planner wouldn't pay you to talk about. If you notice, most keynote speakers talk about broad topics that most all the audience can connect with. In contrast, the workshops or breakout sessions are generally on more niche subjects that appeal to narrower groups of people. As a general rule, keynote speakers are paid and workshop presenters aren't.

In the corporation/association world, speakers generally get paid for things that tangibly affect the company's bottom line. If you can help improve sales, customer service, or company morale, you can get paid.

Your best marketing is a great presentation. Marketing, for a speaker, is telling someone what to think about you until you show up and open your mouth. Someone who is a good marketer but a poor speaker can get booked initially but that won't last. With any service, you still have to be able to deliver. If you're good, word travels. I get most of my new events by people who show up at the events I already do. They hand me their business cards with a smile and request that I come teach at their event. It may seem slow at first, but it picks up pretty quick if you stay on top of it, but always give your best.

One of the best ways to get booked is to get other people to see you live. Any time I go speak somewhere, I always ask myself who is in the area (or at the conference) that has the potential to book me for something else? I know that if I can get them in the room and deliver a great presentation, there's a good chance they'll book me in the future. Why? Look back at the previous point. Your best marketing is a great presentation. So make sure you pack the room with potential decision makers! Book store owners may be in the room, or heads of other events. Like others in the conference room, they may be fans of the topic or specifically looking for speakers for their own events. You never know who might be friends with whom and who might recommend you.

I landed an event in Indianapolis, which gained me a gig in Atlanta and then the Chamber of Commerce in Birmingham, AL the following year. That came from just one event promoter liking, not only my presentation but, how I behaved before and after the event. Remember, you are always under a magnifying glass, so be a proper lady or gentlemen.

Here's one final thing to remember; relationships take time. Getting to speak (and preferably paid to do so) is not an overnight process. It's a slow growth process that takes time. Don't rush that process. If you're committed to not only the craft of writing, add that to the needed category of speaking, but also the marketing and hustle it takes to get started, you can become a frequently booked speaker!

In Tom Antion's Top Ten Ways to Make Money Public Speaking, he has some really great tips.

1. Sell your knowledge – Speaking about something you know a great deal about will go a long way toward getting you paid for what you already know. A book is a great start but don't stop there. You can do audiobooks, Ebooks, videos, CDs, etc. Distributing your knowledge gets your name out there and recognizable which helps you to get more speaking engagements.

2. Get directly paid – This is pretty self-explanatory. When you speak at a business or event they should pay you directly. Oftentimes, you should get a deposit up front, usually around fifty percent, and then the balance can be paid either before the event or the day of.

3. Public Seminars - This is when you promote your own seminar to the public and they buy tickets in order to attend. You can promote them at no cost through your social media, personal website, and email lists. MailChimp is a great service and very inexpensive to use. As you collect fans, email and get subscribers to your emailed blogs to promote yourself.

4. Webinars – I have several writer friends who do this, on occasion, at colleges or through social media advertising (like public seminars) and they have fans sign into Skype conference calls while delivering the seminar. This saves a tremendous amount of money on travel expenses for you along with all kinds of savings for the participants (travel, time, etc.)

WEBCASTS

This is similar to telephone seminars except you are using the Internet instead of a telephone to hold the seminar.

Many professionals speak or give free public seminars to help get clients. Attorneys, doctors, dentists, accountants, real estate agents, lawyers, home builders and many other people from a wide variety of professions give seminars to promote their business and to gain clients directly from the seminars. To do this effectively you must not spend the entire seminar promoting yourself. You must give the participants good information with the idea of establishing yourself or your company as the expert. There is certainly nothing wrong with showing people how complicated things are and even though they can do it themselves, it might not be a wise thing to do. For instance, you could be a plumber giving a seminar on how to remodel your bathroom. You tell the participants every little detail of how to do it and also tell them the perils if they do it wrong. No one will complain that you were just giving a sales pitch, but many will think to themselves, "Maybe this is too much to tackle by myself. Maybe I should hire this person to either help me or do it for me."

Let's talk about how to become a speaker. The first thing I want you to get is the fact that you are already qualified to be a motivational speaker. You don't need any special degrees or qualifications. Your words are good enough

Typically, 20-35% of the audience will make a purchase.

One early secret of success was writing - all the time.

The world is filled with people who believe they have a good story to tell and can motivate others. This means the market is a demand market, not a supply market. You grow demand, starting with a niche where you are known and respected, and grow from there. This also means you won't be paid for a while. Pay comes with demand, which is based on perception, not just talent. Motivational speakers are typically hired because of their story, not because of their speaking or storytelling ability.

Take my friend Christopher. He was on television on SyFy, and wrote a book after we met at a convention. Ok, I talked him into it, but he was a good speaker and I loved his story telling and now he sells out of copies repeatedly at dozens of events every year. Like Christopher, look for events about an expertise you have and start there. You'll have more credibility with audiences that share, or at least respect, your specific background.

Just like your author's platform, earning credibility is easier than ever, between having a YouTube account, Facebook, Twitter, and add in the fact that your cell phone has a video camera which means you can start showing your abilities and building interest in your ideas and talents right now, with just a smart-phone. It takes time to build a following and to earn a reputation sufficiently good enough to have people come looking for you. Your best advantage is your community and network, who may help you get even more attention as they share your posts on their news feed.

Although it's not a quick road to wealth, getting booked as a speaker is totally doable. With perseverance and a lot of hard work, you can make your writing career grow even bigger.

This is a more complex task than we might initially think. What's really being asked of us are two separate questions:

How much value do we bring to the event? (From the conference point of view)

How much is that value worth to us? (From our point of view)

Public speaking is a free market activity. There is no single reference to use for how much to charge. I recommend you read *Confessions of a Public Speaker*; the author earns $30,000 an hour.

In some circles a $500 fee is significant, in other circles that amount is average to low. Study your profession and seek out high profile events. You'll find some conferences charge people $1000 or more to attend for a day, which implies they have sizable budgets for paying speakers. However these budgets come with higher expectations of the profile or fame you need to get that gig.

In the world of conferences and events, there are three factors that make an event valuable: audience, sponsors, and speakers.

Audience: the right audience is valuable to sponsors and the event. The audience must include at least some target customers who might buy products and services from sponsors and vendors, as well as afford the event's ticket prices. A great roster of speakers can attract a valuable audience through speakers' individual networks and promotional efforts, as well as their knowledge.

Sponsors: the right sponsors bring in the money needed to run an event. Without sponsors, an event can't grow or even afford to pay its speakers. A great roster of speakers provides prestige to the event and reassurance to sponsors that the event is credible and will attract an audience.

Speakers: the right speakers bring value to each other. A great roster of speakers provides a community for the speakers to network and learn from each other. Doing conventions you will often have lots of authors sitting in a row sharing insight to the hundreds of fans in the audience.

The role of speakers is to provide credibility, networking opportunities, and reach. That's the value that you provide. Speaking fees scale with the value you provide: the more credibility, networking, and reach you can bring, the greater a fee you can command.

*How to Value Your Role*

The next logical question is, what's the monetary number on the value a speaker provides?

Think about what motivational speaking events or corporate conferences can charge:

150 attendees at $3,000 each: $450,000

5 top-tier sponsors at $25,000 each: $125,000

10 middle-tier sponsors at $12,500 each: $125,000

Attendees at come to hear speakers and, if it is a fan based convention, buy crafts, products, souvenirs, gifts, etc. Thus, the portion of the proceeds above – $450,000 out of the $850,000 gross  is what the speakers are principally responsible for.

If an event had 20 speakers in total. Deduct the cost of hosting the attendee – $1,000 per person and speakers would generate a net revenue for the event of $300,000.

Each individual speaker is responsible for generating $300,000, divided by 20 equals $15,000 in attendee revenue.

That's the cap, the ceiling of what you can reasonably ask for as a speaker in this example, because the profit from sponsorships/ad sales is directly dependent on the event's sales team and not you, and they are solely entitled to that profit for their work. Having speakers at these events brings in more paying attendees and, therefore, creates revenue for those putting on these events. Thus it's reasonable to ask for a percentage of the net revenue, from attendees, as a fee.

*How to Increase Your Fee*

Re-examine what speakers do for events. You provide value through your knowledge, the reason audiences attend. We also provide value through our reach, how many members of our audience we can convince to attend the events we speak at.

To increase our speaking fees, you must improve the value of your knowledge through continued self-improvement; however, from an event perspective, you improve the value of your knowledge through accessibility. Consider offering packages as part of your speaking fee, such as:

- Breakfast/lunch/dinner with you

- one on one short consultations

- book signings with a question and answer portion at the end

By the time you get to this level as a speaker you should be used to this by now.

Say yes to events which offer an equitable exchange of value, and say no to events which take more value than they give.

I hope this explanation of how to set your fee is useful and helpful.

# Conventions, Seminars, and Classes

I know, most writers are introverts by nature, and conventions, especially the big ones, are the worst thing to face. You are probably asking yourself, why would I want to attend a convention?

Sooner or later, you're going to want to interact with people outside of social media and, believe it or not, most of them are just like you; a, possibly shy, introvert who would love to be a writer, artist, or actor, but most of them go to conventions, dressed in their best cosplay costumes, and see the stars they love. These thousands of friendly people can watch out for each other against the 'normal folks' and are usually more fun to be around than if you had to go to a dreaded regular day job, trust me.

At the same time, it can do wonders for your career, especially if you get a chance to pitch your book to a prospective publisher or agent. Think about the fans, and potential fans. Your postcards and business cards are a must have or don't even bother trying to network. Nobody will remember your website URL, or the name of your book, because they're going to be meeting two hundred other people over the duration of the convention that are trying to get them to remember their information as well. Your business card should have your website or blog URL on it, your name, and any contact information that's pertinent. It doesn't hurt if it's a really fancy one. Business cards are cheap. Invest. It doesn't hurt to carry around a couple of your books too, but don't drag fifty to a hundred pounds of books around downtown Georgia in the heat like I have a few times. Not only will it wear you out, you could ruin expensive luggage. You can't give a book to everyone you meet, but you never know who you're going to run into.

For the small press or self-published author, you can lug your wares to the convention, rent booth space, and sell some books directly to your fans. That's what you are supposed to do, and, if you are a big enough name, you will get comped a booth (you'll get it for free) if you are part of the draw for the crowd. It's good for the ego to meet and talk to people who enjoy your work, and at the same time build brand loyalty.

## Conventions

I've done hundreds of conventions. Some of them have become expected annual events that I go to again and again. I enjoy the types of events I go to as much as any other fan of horror, sci-fi, or whatever major type I attend, but I strongly suggest a word of caution. **These are not vacations.** You are at these events to make a living, and you are constantly in 'on' mode. Conduct yourself professionally because a wide variety of people are watching you. You not only have fans seeing what you're doing but you also may have event planners from other conventions who might be looking at you to book for other gigs. You may even meet stars and producers that can pass your name onto other people. Of course, enjoy your time there, but balance is critical and know that someone is always watching.

### *Promoting Your Work at Conventions*

Science fiction and fantasy conventions (known affectionately by attendees as the abbreviation 'cons') are a great place for authors of those genres to promote their work to readers. Most cons are 'fan' conventions in which attendees, including program participants, generally attend primarily to participate in the convention experience. This fan convention culture is unlike higher-profile, for-profit media shows where nearly all program participants are there to sell or promote themselves or their work and where attendees are primarily audience members.

The big ones, like Comic Con, DragonCon, and Scarefest, just to name a few, are based on a wider range of comic books, roleplaying games, music, science fiction or horror, and paranormal. Crowds can contain over 70,000 attendees over the three or four day weekend. Very specific ones, like Walker Stalker Con or Supernatural, are based off of particular television shows like *The Walking Dead* and *Supernatural* and bring in thousands of fans eager to meet their beloved stars. It is also a great place to be an author of any related topic, if you can secure a booth in the vendor rooms, or better yet, become a panelist and speaker at them. I feel very fortunate that the genres I am most known for take me to heavily attended events and I make a good deal of money and get lots of exposure for my new books. You also gain hundreds of new fans. If you have, by this point, sold a decent amount of books at shops during a book signing, trust me, this is the same thing but on steroids, if your book is in anyway related to these kinds of conventions. You may have a ling of fans of the genre eagerly throwing money at you. I have had it happen at several large conventions, especially DragonCon, after a talk I gave on a paranormal book I wrote. It sounds thrilling and stressful, right? Well, it is. Hand-selling your books at conventions gets easier only with experience, but also with more titles on your table. When you increase your amount of titles, and the type of content, you are increasing your opportunities to appeal to different tastes, and you will eventually get a feel for what works best for you since every writer usually has a special genre they excel at.

Set your table up to look nice and pay attention to how others set up. Although not a book seller, a friend of mine used to work retail as a manager in a mall and quit to do her own business, Poking Dead Things. Morgana Grimm became good friends with me and taught me that a vendor at events needs to focus on displays, and how you set up your wares. Signs and lighting are important. People don't want to ask questions, they are shy or don't want to be a bother, so use signs and cards as your "silent salesperson", as Morgana calls it. It gives your customer the information that they may be looking for but don't want to ask. You need to be right there in case they have other questions though also.

Look at how the pros do it. Think of yourself as a traveling store.

Practice your set-up at home, use display racks, especially the collapsible ones. Bring a nice tablecloth. Make sure your prices are clearly visible and you have some bookmarks, or other "swag" type merchandise, like stickers, to give away. Get a vinyl banner and a stand to go with it; it'll help attract people and make you look professional. I strongly recommend you use both your book cover and an image of yourself on the banner as well as on your business card or postcards so that people who meet you remember who wrote the book, especially if people who are in a position to help market you stop by and grab your contact information.

Prepare your book pitch, but also try to come up with something you can say to people who come up to your booth or are just walking by, even if it's just "Hey, do you like (insert your particular genre) books?" Not everyone is there to buy. Keep in mind that they've paid to get into the convention, as well as travel and food expenses. The attendees, after they buy a few famous peoples autographs, may not have a lot of money left.

Don't pester people, just say hello, give them the pitch if they're interested, and answer any questions they might have. At the table, never sit down, always stand up if at all possible. Enabling potential readers to have a personal encounter with you and your ideas can often make or break an attendee's interest. Don't look bored. You're one hundred percent of the sales force behind your book. You know it best and have the passion behind it, unlike anyone else. Know your neighbors and co-panelists; they can be helpful. You tend to get to know one another if you keep doing similar shows. They'll guard your stuff while you go get lunch, run to the restroom, or take an urgent call. Do the same for them. Build relationships. Take it a step further and get to know their products, maybe you can direct some customers their way and they will do it for you too. The more you do the same convention, or others like it, you may get to see the same people again and again, so leave a good impression.

Keep in mind Murphy's Law; prepare for the worst. You can't really prepare for disaster, but you can prepare psychologically. It would have helped me out the time when a guy put his drink on top of my stack of art prints and ruined all of them. Another one spilled his soda on t-shirts and books that had to be tossed. Not everyone is mindful that your table is, essentially, a store. Keep in mind our previous section on store signings and your appearance also. Keep a small package of breath mints and cologne on you, don't be the stereotype of the unwashed gamer.

*Speaking at conventions*

By now you are used to public speaking and know everything right? I thought I was pretty at ease, until one time at DragonCon I was pulled up onto a panel on vampires, and asked to sit down with two respected colleagues, and yet I hesitated. It was my friend and mentor, Michelle Belanger, and, at the time, new acquaintance, Rosemary Ellen Guiley, along with four other famous award winning authors like Chelsea Quinn Yarbro. It can be very intimidating. It was also the first time I spoke in front of over two hundred faces. I recall Michelle telling me I would do just fine, and I did, but I will never forget it! As of this writing, I have been a repeat guest of the Horror Track at DragonCon for six years, so I must be doing something right. I am going to share with you tips on these trips that should help new writers traveling to their first convention.

When you're on the panel, relax, use the tips we covered already in the chapter on public speaking, be prepared, and be engaging. Talk more about the other authors' books that are on the panel with you, and usually, they will do the same in respect back. Writers who talk incessantly about their own books risk coming across as egotistical jerks.

I have found the audience will really get into it, and many will seek you out after the panel to ask questions, which is the perfect time to tell them you have a booth/table where you're selling your books at, or if you have some behind the table (most panels frown on having you sell at the panel talk, that's why they sell booth spaces). I have had a lot of fans from all over the country approach me and excitedly say they came just to meet me or see me again. Engage them in conversation about the convention. Ask them questions, like are they enjoying themselves. Make them feel special and not like they are there just to buy your book. The longer you talk to someone, the more likely they are to walk away with your product. Engage with them, don't treat them like an animal of prey. People sense that in your demeanor and your reputation will erode, sometimes to the point of not being asked back. Be friendly. Be humble. Just listen to the horror stories about how William Shatner, who has been notorious for showing up late and asking for extravagant things, acted at a few events and do not be a prima donna. Places like DragonCon and ComicCon are crazy expensive, with travel, hotel, and food. I know deep down you are going to do mental calculations every few hours seeing your funds disappear and it is tempting to feel like you have to sell hard to the attendees to make it back, but trust me, it is highly unlikely that you will sell enough books at a convention to cover your costs, so don't get too caught up in that. Especially not the first few times you are there. Usually, at best you break even and make new connections that triple their value later on down the road. Aside from the mental health aspect of meeting/hanging out with fellow writers, the main benefit is that you've made some personal connections with new readers, who are then more likely to become the kind of fans who will sustain your career in the long-term. They'll come back next year to see if your next book is out.

Another attending professional shared his wisdom on DragonCon:

"Cooperate with other authors. Buying booths or tables at the massive conventions like DragonCon is cost-prohibitive, where costs for a booth run into the thousands of dollars. When you split those costs with fellow authors, however, the fees become much more reasonable.

The cost of a $3,000 booth split ten ways is a bargain when you consider that 80,000 fans with red-hot money in their pockets will filter past over the course of a four-day weekend.

So round up some of your author friends, form some sort of collective, and take a convention by storm."

Having several people share the booth is good for other reasons as well. You can give each other breaks to get food or use the restroom and know that someone will be manning your booth so potential customers don't think it's abandoned.

Another trick I use when speaking at conventions is to get business cards from other speakers and stay in touch with them. Sometimes they ask me to attend other events they know of that I haven't heard of. Strike up conversations often, you never know when you might be talking to a potential reader, or make a positive impression on someone who might mention your name to other attendees or their friends.

Your aim is to increase your visibility and to interest attendees in your work. I've learned a good deal of ways in which you can best make a good impression at conventions.

Don't insist on a free pass just because you're a published author, however, if you get booked as a VIP, ask to know ahead what that notoriety gets you. Will they supply you with travel expense and/or a hotel room?

Conventions always cost you something. Never assume, even if you get compensated for the trip, a table, and a hotel room, that it was free. You do need to keep in mind that it costs your time. You are a writer and while doing promotion you aren't writing your next book. Conventions are fun, but never lose sight that they are part of the job. Treat it seriously. You will rarely make back your investment in a table unless you already have some name recognition. There are advantages of being a guest speaker, and being on panels, of course. The benefits of exposure and networking opportunities with other authors are valuable assets.

Look at the proposed convention program and learn who else is attending; you never know who you will make friends with.

A key point that I want to stress is make a good impression, not a bad one. Write positive convention reports on your web site, blog, or social media.

Do NOT act in a way that is likely to give you a reputation for being demanding or uncooperative.

Another thing to consider is donating copies of your work to the convention. Conventions use donations in various ways: for charity auctions, as motivational giveaways for volunteers, distributed as freebies in convention packets, and several other ways. This is both a good way to get your work out to your potential audience and to enhance a positive image with the convention.

Do not demand payment for signatures or photos unless the con has indicated that it is their standard policy (rare for fan-run non-media conventions).

*Being a Good Program Participant*

When you are asked to be part of a panel be prepared to discuss the topic of the panel, possibly making notes or doing research before the convention.

Do not over prepare – remember that you are not going to be the only person speaking on the topic.

Do not have a stack of your books sitting in front of you while on the panel. It is best if you have the books under a table and let people ask you about them after the panel. If you have a booth at the event make sure to have your books there and try to get people to stop by it as they peruse the convention.

Do mention your work briefly in your introduction, but mainly mention why you are interested in the panel topic.

Do not talk solely about your own work.

Engage with the other panelists and talk about the subject of the panel. The more entertaining, informative, and engaged you are, the more likely it is that someone in the audience will want to find your books.

One of the biggest pieces of advice on how to behave well is if you are not the moderator of the panel you are on, do not take over the job of the moderator by calling on people in the audience. Do not interrupt other panelists, or otherwise be a prima donna.

*Making a Good Impression on Other Industry Professionals*

While at larger conventions you can sometimes make some business connections. Fan conventions are not business oriented.

Never be pushy to other writers to get them to impart secrets. Let them get to know you and like you. Don't ask other writers to get you in touch with their agents. If you truly connect with them they will do it for you later on.

Try your best to keep track of who you met and who introduced you. If you later query an agent or editor whom you met or were introduced to at a con, you can then mention specifics to jog their memory, like saying to them that you enjoyed meeting them last year at the Con.

You can build connections any time you meet someone who is a good fit for you. I do it all the time. Because of the friends I have made, I've come to know people online through Twitter, Facebook, and other social media. Make sure to let fans know, at the end of panels, how to add you on social media.

If you are creative and persistent, but without seeming pushy or desperate, you can reach the people you need to reach with your work. You may not think, initially, you have made a deep inroad into your future, but the small steps listed here are huge in making a seriously good impression on everyone you encounter. The long game is vital and you will leave a good image in their minds.

I've made some great friends at the convention circuit; a lot of television and film stars who I can chat with yearly, some of whom were stars I admired in movies or television shows that I never dreamed I would ever call "friend". I never would have thought that I would occasionally call them up to just catch up on how they have been, let alone publish the biography of one of them. Treat them as human beings and they will appreciate you. They get goo-goo-eyed enough daily as it is. Stars tend to treat attending professionals a bit more like 'one of them' because both of you do the same thing for a huge part of your publicity and you both fully understand the grueling schedule of travel, long hours on the bus, at train stations and airports, the sea of faces and pawing fans. Of course, we love our fans, but after years of doing it, you do develop a bit of an armor against the possibility of wackjobs. Take for example how actor Norman Reedus was bitten by a female fan when he appeared at Walker Stalker Con and she asked for a photo with him!

## Seminars and Teaching a Class at an Event

As a business owner, and you *are* a business even if that business is just one book that you've published, or if you are an author of several books, you have expertise in your particular industry. A great way to attract buyers into your business is to run a special event that fits the theme of your work. If you do horror, push your work at a local library around Halloween. A friend of mine writes about herbal remedies and the uses of plants and so she did a series of educational classes, especially in the Spring time when people are just starting to get outside and plants are blooming. Find what matches what you do, and grow your presence from there. Save articles posted online and use them on your website; put the link on your social media to highlight the favorable review you have had.

You can even profit directly from holding your own events. Charge for admission or for products you sell that relate to your book. You can do this at bookstores, all you have to do is show up and present, and it spreads your fame to other cities. Speak at local libraries and work your way around to the surrounding states. Book signings at stores while in the same city at the same time, just to get more out of your trip! Bookstores and libraries aren't your only options. Find stores or other locations and events that fit your genre and ask if you can do a book signing, lecture, or workshop there.

At some of the events I do the store owners will pay for my meals and hotel since they get traffic in larger numbers; a captive audience that buys from them as well, so they recoup the money and get people to come into their shop. I've tried this myself when I ran a store in my hometown and I brought a few authors, which our store carried, in. Good networking spreads like wildfire, if you mix this in with trips to conventions, you are well on your way.

# Afterword

Every single sale has a ripple effect and touches others like a domino effect. Think big and small combined, tactically. Do not only think in terms of large chains for your signings, but in smaller aspects, such as in quaint shops and libraries. Never overlook an opportunity. Word of mouth matters just as much if not more.

I don't tell you guys to do anything that, I, myself, have been unwilling to do. I sincerely hope this book has encouraged you to do what you always dreamed of and that my reality check does not dash your dreams. We need our dreams to keep us going, but with common sense to keep us from making terrible mistakes that could otherwise prevent us from having the success we seek.

As self-publishing authors know, you must wear many hats, overcome a lot of steps, and dedicate yourself to producing a top-notch book from cover to cover, not to mention building your author platform.

As in any field, those who succeed are those who persevere. It is my opinion that the most important trait for any writer is determination. I am always willing to share what I learn and if you have more questions, don't hesitate to reach me. Now, get out a pen and paper, or turn on your computer, and start your career as an author. Best of luck to you!

Best sellers by the author:

Embracing the Darkness

Understanding Dark Subcultures A Decade of Darkness

Special tenth anniversary edition with expanded material

CORVIS NOCTURNUM

Foreword by Michelle Belanger
Afterword by Gavin Baddeley

# The Sixth Millionaire

BY THE AUTHOR OF UNLOCKING THE SECRETS
OF CONTROL, WEALTH AND POWER

## E. R. Vernor

E.R. Vernor

The History of

# Vampires

*Introduction by Rosemary Ellen Guiley*

# THE BOOK OF THE DEAD

Death and Mourning Through the Ages

E.R. Vernor 'Corvis Nocturnum'

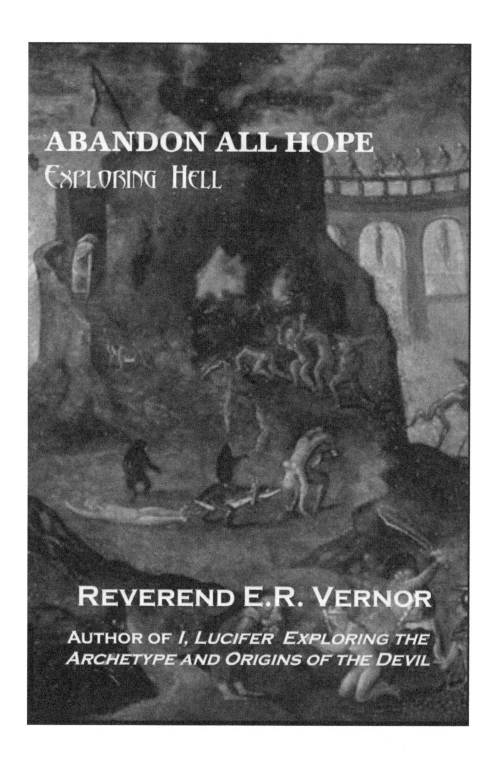

# ABANDON ALL HOPE
## Exploring Hell

# REVEREND E.R. VERNOR

AUTHOR OF *I, LUCIFER  EXPLORING THE
ARCHETYPE AND ORIGINS OF THE DEVIL*

# The Buddha and The Devil
## Two Paths One Journey

Authors and motivational speakers

E.R. Vernor 'Corvis Nocturnum

and

Hokyo Joshua Routhier

UNLOCKING THE SECRETS

OF CONTROL, WEALTH AND POWER

CONTROL OVER YOUR LIFE

WEALTH BEYOND JUST FINANCIAL

POWER TO CHANGE YOUR WORLD

E.R. VERNOR

Foreword by Brian J. Cano

# LILITH

## From Ancient Lore To Modern Culture

E.R. Vernor

*Author of I Lucifer: Exploring the Origins and Archetype of the Devil*

SUPERNATURAL
PLACES OF EUROPE

Author of the *Eerie America Travel Guide of the Macabre* series

E.R. Vernor

Made in the USA
Middletown, DE
08 September 2024